PLAY BLACKJACK TO WIN

PLAYING BLACKJACK TO WIN

by

Roger R. Baldwin

Wilbert E. Cantey

Herbert Maisel

James P. McDermott

CARDOZA PUBLISHING

FREE ONLINE GAMING NEWSLETTERS!
www.cardozabooks.com

Sign up for Avery Cardoza's FREE email gaming newsletters and receive three great products: Avery Cardoza's Poker Newsletter, Avery Cardoza's Gambling Newsletter and Avery Cardoza's Online Gaming Newsletter. Our newsletters are packed with tips, expert strategies, news, special discounts, free money sign-up bonuses for online sites, prepublication discounts, poker and gaming tournament schedules, and words of wisdom from the world's top experts and players. It's FREE! Sign up now!

www.cardozabooks.com

See Free Book Offer On Page 137

Cardoza Publishing is the foremost gaming and gambling publisher in the world with a library of over 200 up-to-date and easy-to-read books and strategies. These authoritative works are written by the top experts in their fields and with more than 10 million books in print, represent the best-selling and most popular gaming books anywhere.

Copyright © 2008 by Cardoza Publishing
— All Rights Reserved —

Bibliographic Note
This Cardoza Edition, first published in 2008 is a reprint of
the original title, *Playing Blackjack to Win*, first published by
M. Barrows and Company in 1957. The current volume also includes a
preface, foreword and an introductory note specially
prepared for this edition.

Library of Congress Catalog No: 2008927154
ISBN 10: 1-58042-251-9
ISBN 13: 978-158042-251-2

Visit our new web site (www.cardozabooks.com) or write us
for a full list of books, advanced and computer strategies.

CARDOZA PUBLISHING
P.O. Box 98115, Las Vegas, NV 89193
Toll Free Phone (800)577-WINS
email: cardozabooks@aol.com
www.cardozabooks.com

TABLE OF CONTENTS

Preface to the New Edition 7

Foreword to the New Edition 9

Introduction to the New Edition 11

A Monumental Idea Gains Momentum 13

Blackjack is Finally Solved! 16

Charles Van Doren Enters the Picture 17

The Four Horseman Start an Avalanche 18

The Four Horsemen Reappear 21

The Four Horsemen Since Aberdeen 23

Foreword 31

Introduction 35

The Game of Blackjack 38

Definition of the Game 41

The Rules of Blackjack 42

The Best Strategy for Drawing or Standing 48

The Best Strategy for Doubling Down 58

The Best Strategy for Splitting Pairs 63

Blackjack — The Fairest Game 67

The Best Strategy in Action 75

A Simplified Strategy for the Casual Player 78

The Price of Not Following the Best Strategy 80

Variations in Casino Rules 87

Using the Exposed Cards to Improve Your
Chances 94

A Special Word to "The Sport" 104

The Sport's Options 105

The Home Game 107

Rules for the Home Game 109

General Principles for the Player 112

Comparison of the Strategies for the Home and
    Casino Games 119

The Player's Strategy for Drawing and Standing on
    Soft Hands 121

The Player's Strategy for Doubling Down 123

The Player's Strategy for Splitting Pairs 123

The Player's Strategy in Trying for Bonuses 125

How to Play the Deal 126

The Dealer's Advantage in the Home Game 127

The Value of the Deal 127

Appendix: Rules on Irregularities 128

The Home Game 129

The Casino Game 130

Special Detachable Summary for Casino Reference 134

The Simplified Strategy 134

PREFACE
TO THE
NEW EDITION

You are holding in your hands the most influential book in the history of the game of blackjack. When the now extremely rare *Playing Blackjack to Win* was initially released in 1957, it was the first time *ever* that the correct winning strategies for blackjack were published in book form.

More than half a century later, Cardoza Publishing is proud to re-release this classic volume. Millions of blackjack players around the world can now see where it all began and understand how this breakthrough work influenced not only all future professional blackjack players, but the growth of Las Vegas itself.

This landmark book was akin, in its historic achievement, to the great European explorers who, through countless expeditions, sought out the original source of the Nile and finally achieved that goal in the mid-nineteenth century. John Hanning Speke, on an expedition led by Sir Richard Francis Burton, achieved that goal in 1858. Nearly 100 years later, another monumental discovery solved a bewildering problem—the mathematically correct way to beat the game of blackjack. The Four Horsemen—Baldwin, Cantey, Maisel and McDermott—are the giants who changed a landscape.

In the interest of maintaining the flavor of this historic book, we have not altered the grammar or style of the original version; however, we have added vintage photographs and redesigned the book for modern presentation. We also have included new material from blackjack legends Edward O. Thorp and Arnold Snyder.

If you're a true fan of the game of blackjack, this very rare book is one you need in your collection.

AVERY CARDOZA
PUBLISHER

FOREWORD
TO THE
NEW EDITION

In 1958, I was a new Ph.D. teaching in the U.C.L.A. mathematics department. My wife, Vivian, and I were going to Las Vegas over the Christmas break for a non-gambling vacation. However, Professor Robert Sorgenfrey told me about a blackjack strategy with a remarkably small expected rate of loss. It was published in 1956 (by the authors of this book) in the *Journal of the American Statistical Association* as "The Optimum Strategy in Blackjack." It was approximately best assuming either a full deck or that one didn't keep track of the cards played.

Arriving in Las Vegas, I sat down at a blackjack table, and held in the palm of my hand a tiny strategy card (the "basic strategy") constructed from the information in the *JASA* article. It looked a lot like the chart in the back of this book, but was much smaller—the size of two postage stamps.

After slowly losing $8.50 of my $10 stake, while the other players at my table were being devastated, I retired. But I started thinking and, back at U.C.L.A., I carefully read the *JASA* article. Almost immediately I visualized a ten-parameter space with each parameter corresponding to the quantity of one value of card. I felt intuitively sure that, were I to carry out the authors' calculations for each "point" in this space, i.e., the subset of the pack of cards, I would find whole regions where the casino's edge was substantially shifted, sometimes perhaps, even greatly in the player's favor.

I wrote Roger Baldwin and asked to borrow the authors' hand calculations. Cartons of lab notebooks with tens of thousands of computations arrived a few weeks later. The *JASA* paper plus the notebooks let me quickly master the authors' approximate calculation of basic strategy. Meanwhile, I accepted a teaching position at M.I.T. and, with the aid of their IBM 704 computer, was able to calculate a more accurate basic strategy and to do this for many subsets of cards. What I learned launched the modern card counting era. Though I worked from the *JASA* paper and not this book, I realized afterwards when I read this book that the authors might very well have come to similar conclusions if they had done or redone their work a few years later when high speed computers were becoming available.

With their *JASA* paper and this subsequent book, the authors planted the seed for the blackjack revolution and the modern era of card counting. That seed triggered a cascade of ever widening consequences that have affected many lives, not least mine among them. I am indebted to the authors for sharing with me, almost fifty years ago, the details of their work. To paraphrase Issac Newton, "If I have seen farther than others, it is because I stood on the shoulders of four giants."

EDWARD O. THORP
AUTHOR OF BEAT THE DEALER

INTRODUCTION
TO THE
NEW EDITION

The Four Horsemen of Aberdeen: How Four GIs Beat the Game That Stumped the Experts

For the first two hundred years of blackjack's history, as the game became popular in casinos throughout the world, neither the players nor the casinos had any idea of the right way to play it. Among the card experts and experienced gamblers alike, there was wide disagreement over the optimal strategy. In fact, no one even knew the house edge on the game—*or whether there was a house edge*. By the mid-twentieth century, all of the other popular house-banked casino games—craps, roulette, baccarat, faro, keno, the wheel of fortune, even the slot machines—had been mathematically analyzed in depth. But not blackjack. The casinos offered the game because it was popular. They assumed there was a house edge because they made money on it. But everyone agreed that it was just too complex to analyze.

Then a series of improbable events changed the history of the game forever. According to Roger Baldwin, a twenty-three-year-old private in the U.S. Army who'd had a passion for "getting the edge" in games: "When the weather got cold that winter at the Aberdeen

Proving Grounds in 1953, some poker games sprang up in the barracks. It was draw poker. Money was in play. The first time I sat down at this game, we were playing dealer's choice and someone said, 'Let's play blackjack.' And then some discussion occurred on the rules. I had played some blackjack in high school, though not for money. And the rules for the home game are quite different, particularly in the fact that the dealer has flexibility in how to play his hand. Then somebody said, 'In Nevada, the dealer has to draw on 16 or less and stand on 17 or more.'"

That comment by a fellow soldier turned out to be a critical moment for the game of casino blackjack. As luck would have it, Baldwin wasn't your average buck private; he was a buck private who had recently earned a master's degree in statistics from Columbia University. It occurred to Roger that this restriction on the dealer's actions made blackjack a very different game from poker. With no bluffing and a fore-knowledge of how the dealer had to play his hand, it seemed to him that there should be a mathematically optimal way for the player to play his own hand based on the dealer's upcard. It also dawned on him that a mathematical analysis of blackjack might pay off. "In the case of blackjack, you couldn't really say who had the edge. We knew the casinos were in the business of making money, but it was an open question. After learning that the dealers in Las Vegas had a fixed strategy, I thought maybe we could beat this game. I kept the idea to myself for a while, just mulling the thing over and looking at the possibilities. You might call it a gold rush in slow motion."

A MONUMENTAL IDEA GAINS MOMENTUM

Baldwin wasn't sure of exactly how to do it, but he spent the next couple of months working out the formulas for all of the problems that would have to be solved in order to devise an accurate blackjack strategy. No one told him that, for two hundred years, the game had been considered too complex to solve. He simply set out to solve it. When he finally came up with the methodology required to analyze the game, he realized that it would take a lot of work.

He talked to his sergeant about using the office calculators in the army analytical laboratory where they worked. No problem. As it turned out, this sergeant— Wilbert Cantey—also had a master's degree and was a gambler with a particular passion for blackjack himself.

According to Cantey, "I had a lot of blackjack in me. I played blackjack as a kid, under the house in South Carolina. We would play for pennies. That's how I got kicked out of the seminary years later. The Dean of the Seminary said, 'Young man, I've seen you in the pool hall and I've seen you playing cards, and you seem to be a great pool player. However, I don't think you need to major in religion. I think you better look for your next best subject.' And my next best subject was math. I had graduated from high school at fifteen with honors. I'd developed an intuitive strategy for playing blackjack in private games, but in those games the dealer could do anything he wanted to, and the deal went from one person to another. The game of blackjack is quite different when it's structured as in Las

Vegas, and you have a fixed dealer and rules for how the dealer must play. I jumped at the opportunity to analyze it in terms of probabilities."

Baldwin then recruited a couple of other privates with master's degrees in mathematics who worked in the same office—Herbert Maisel and James McDermott—to help solve the riddle of blackjack. And for the next year and a half, these four men spent most of their free time—which they estimated at a thousand man-hours—punching numbers into the Monroe and Marchant desk calculators the Army provided in the Aberdeen research lab.

According to Baldwin, "It started in October of 1953 and by March of 1955, the calculations were pretty much over. The first focus was on drawing and standing. Then we went on to doubling down in January of 1954. At the time we began this analysis, we had only very cursory information on rules and we thought you could only double down on a total of eleven. Then in June of 1954, I went to Las Vegas and I spent a week going to the sixteen casinos that were operating—eight in the downtown area and eight on the Strip. That trip to Nevada was a revelation because I learned that you could double down on *any* two cards. That meant a lot more calculations. I also found out that we had to do part of our pair splitting analysis over because we hadn't known you could double down after splitting."

A thousand hours of number crunching? As Herb Maisel remarked, "We were in the Army. There was nothing else to do." McDermott explained: "Part of it was just finding something interesting to do and this was a pretty good bunch of guys to work with.

There was also the challenge—not so much the mathematical challenge but the challenge of being the first to solve this problem... I'm not sure exactly when this happened but we began to look at what the card experts said. I don't think we knew anything about Scarne then, but we knew about Culbertson and Goren—they were the card experts—and it was obvious that their blackjack strategies were different from each other. It didn't make any sense, and we realized that nobody had ever figured it out."

Maisel admits that he was also attracted to the profit potential of the game. "It definitely occurred to us while doing all this work that maybe, if we could come up with the best way to play, we could actually make some money. There was a lot of talk about that. It was a real incentive to us. Also, this was a real world application of mathematics. Statistics was the thing that interested me, and here we had a problem that looked solvable. I have to be honest—if I knew how many times we'd have to redo our calculations, I'm not sure I would have bought into it. I think we all underestimated how much work it would be. But once we got going and we could see that we were building something that made sense and worked well, it kept me going."

Another thing that kept them all going was that the strategy they were discovering was so unlike the previously published strategies of the experts. According to Herb Maisel, "I think at one point we actually got a little scared because our strategy was so different from what had been published before. Taking advantage of things like splitting pairs and doubling down, for instance, showed a lot more value than I think anyone had expected. That was one of the reasons we were always double-checking our work and plotting our results. We wanted to be sure before we said this is the best way to play."

"What surprised me," said Jim McDermott, "were the standing totals in given situations. Standing on a total of 12, for example—no one had ever suggested in any of the books that this would be correct."

Baldwin concurred. "I initially felt a lot of encouragement about the prospect of making money from our project because our early results were very counterintuitive."

BLACKJACK IS FINALLY SOLVED!

The Four Horsemen ultimately accomplished what all the game experts had failed to do for more than two centuries.

In June of 1955, Roger Baldwin submitted a first draft of an article on their findings to the *Journal of the American Statistical Association*. After some revisions, the article was published in the September 1956 issue of the ASA journal as the lead article. The fact that a professional journal of such prestige had published their article was a considerable coup for them. None of them had a Ph.D., nor were any of them teaching statistics in major universities, as was the norm for contributors to the ASA journal. They were just enlisted men in the U.S. Army. The fact that their submission was the lead article in the issue where it appeared was icing on the cake. It became one of the most talked about articles ever to appear in that publication, and according to the Library of Congress, became one of the most photocopied articles to ever appear in a technical journal.

The general public, however, didn't read statistical journals, and no one other than statisticians knew that an accurate basic strategy for the game of casino blackjack had been developed. Roger wanted to publish their findings for a bigger audience—an audience of players who could actually use their findings in the casinos.

In November of 1956, they found a small New York publisher, Barrows and Company, that gave them a contract to produce the book within the next year. Jim McDermott and Roger Baldwin were the primary authors of *Playing Blackjack to Win,* with Roger, according to Jim, writing more than half of it. The manuscript was finished sometime around June of 1957. Then, to sweeten the book's sales prospects, Roger got Charles Van Doren to write the Foreword. Most people today probably do not recognize the name Charles Van Doren, but in 1957—the year their book was published—he was a media star.

CHARLES VAN DOREN ENTERS THE PICTURE

In January of 1957, at the age of 30, Van Doren had appeared for the first time on a popular television quiz show called *Twenty-One.* He had a master's degree in astrophysics as well as a doctorate in English from Columbia University. *Twenty-One*, essentially, was a test of knowledge that required contestants to attempt to outscore each other by answering successively more difficult questions. Van Doren's winning streak was so phenomenal, and the knowledge he exhibited on such a wide range of subjects so astonishing, that he made the cover of *Time* magazine in February 1957 (and later *Life* magazine's cover), and went on to win $129,000 on the show in just two months, an incredible sum at that time. (Little did anyone know that, within two years, Charles Van Doren would be the subject of one of the biggest scandals in the history of television. In a U.S. Congressional investigation, Van Doren admitted that he had been supplied with answers by the producers of the TV show for the questions he was asked on *Twenty-One*.)

According to Roger, "When I was growing up, the Van Doren family lived on the same block as me in Greenwich Village. Charles was four years older than me and he went to the same elementary school. I remember lying in bed at the age of eleven, trying to get to sleep, and Charles would be playing the clarinet. It was beautiful. So it was natural for me to ask him to write the Foreword for our book. As a gesture of friendship, we bought him a small gift—I think it was valued at about seventy-five dollars. Of course, it wiped out about 30 percent of our royalties!"

THE FOUR HORSEMAN START AN AVALANCHE

Playing Blackjack to Win was finally published as a spiral-bound book in the fall of 1957, with a retail price of $1.75. It was the first book to present an accurate basic strategy for casino blackjack. Ever. The first edition of *Playing Blackjack to Win* was printed in an edition of 5,000 copies. As it has never been reprinted until now, first edition copies are collector's items.

The strategy devised by these four GIs has since been published in millions of books. Hundreds of thousands of blackjack players all over the world depend on it. It has rocked the casino industry to its core. Yet, these four men who bucked two hundred years of history and did what all the experts said could not be done remain relatively unknown to all but a handful of hardcore blackjack aficionados who comprehend the magnitude and Herculean effort of their achievement. It was their work that ultimately led to the development of the powerful card counting systems that were not only responsible for millions of dollars in profits for professional blackjack players for decades to come, but caused an unprecedented boom in the popularity of blackjack and the expansion of the casino industry worldwide.

In addition to the first accurate basic strategy, *Playing Blackjack to Win* also contained the first legitimate card counting strategy ever published in a chapter titled "Using the Exposed Cards to Improve Your Chances." Prior to this book, the only other book to mention the possibility of a blackjack player altering his strategy based on cards that have already come out of the deck was Mickey MacDougall's 1944 *MacDougall on Dice and Cards*—a book referenced in their 1956 article in the ASA journal—but MacDougal never provided any actual strategy for the game. According to Baldwin, "The term 'card counting' wasn't used back then. There was another interesting term that was used by someone I talked to out in Las Vegas—he called it 'dead-ending.' The concept was that with a single deck they'd wait until only fifteen cards were left and then change the bets."

In 1958, the same year he earned his Ph.D. in mathematics from UCLA, Edward O. Thorp contacted Roger Baldwin. Thorp had seen the blackjack strategy article in the ASA journal, and he wanted to know if he could see the workbooks the authors had kept with all of their data. Baldwin sent Thorp all of their notebooks—reams of data they'd collected from their hand calculators in order to develop their strategy. The following year, Thorp contacted them again, this time with errata on their 1956 ASA journal article. Most of the errata were minor typos or slight errors in numbers or notation, but they appreciated the fact that he had studied their findings more deeply than anyone else. Then, in 1960, they got another letter from Ed Thorp, in which he told them that based on the work they had done, he had used an IBM 704 computer at MIT to develop a method for getting a substantial edge against the house in the game of casino blackjack.

The rest is history. Thorp's *Beat the Dealer* was published in 1962 and became a bestseller. The world of casino gambling hasn't been the same since.

Although no one knew it at the time, the basic strategy published by Baldwin, Cantey, Maisel, and McDermott, actually did provide a player advantage over the house in the blackjack game they had analyzed, which was the game that was being dealt in Las

Vegas at that time—single deck, dealer stands on soft 17, double down on any two cards, and double down after splitting. According to their analysis in *Playing Blackjack to Win,* the house edge over a player using their strategy was about six-tenths of a percent. In the 1966 edition of *Beat the Dealer,* however, with a more comprehensive computer analysis of their strategy, Ed Thorp determined that—despite a few inconsequential errors on borderline plays—their basic strategy as they published it actually provided "a player edge of 0.09%." And this edge over the house that their basic strategy provided did not include any of the potential gains from the card counting advice they also included in the book.

Edward O. Thorp acknowledges in *Beat the Dealer* that it was the painstaking work of Baldwin, Cantey, Maisel, and McDermott that ultimately led to his own computer research into the game, and to his development of the first powerful card counting systems. And in 1965, in *The Casino Gambler's Guide,* Dr. Allan N. Wilson called their book "a masterpiece" and dubbed them "The Four Horsemen of Aberdeen," a nickname that has stuck with them to this day.

THE FOUR HORSEMEN REAPPEAR

The Four Horsemen never wrote anything more on the game of blackjack and, for decades, blackjack experts, aficionados, and professional players had wondered what had become of them. Then, in March of 2007, out of the blue, I got an email from James McDermott and learned through subsequent emails that the Four Horsemen still got together periodically to discuss those days back in Aberdeen.

I had a hundred questions for these guys, and on October 23, 2007, I finally got my questions answered. My publisher and editor, Avery Cardoza, and I spent an entire day with the Four Horsemen. We talked about the state of blackjack today, the casino industry, the Internet, card counting, poker, what they'd been doing for the past fifty years, but mostly about those years they spent together at the Aberdeen Proving Grounds, changing the world of casino gambling as we know it. I'm happy to report that the Four Horsemen of Aberdeen were witty and sharp as tacks.

Did the Army actually know they had spent years employing government equipment for the purpose of analyzing casino blackjack? Yes. They said that both their civilian and military supervisors were aware of what they were doing and never had any objections. In fact, they posted a chart on the office wall where they worked plotting their results and showing their progress. They did all of their work on the black-jack project in their off-duty hours, and they had a lot of off-duty hours to fill. In fact, according to Jim McDermott, "There's no way we could have done it if we weren't in the Army."

I had never even seen a photograph of the Four Horsemen before. Why did their book not include a photo of the authors on the back cover, as was typical for books at that time, just as in the present? According to Herb Maisel, "Barrows actually asked us to take pictures to promote the book. Everything was going swimmingly until they saw the pictures. They decided that Wil's picture on the back of the book as an author would hurt sales. Until they got the pictures, they didn't know Wil was black."

THE FOUR HORSEMEN SINCE ABERDEEN

The Four Horsemen of Aberdeen never got into serious gambling. They went on to success in various fields where their talents in math and their passion for problem-solving were valued.

Roger Baldwin moved to New York City after leaving the Army in 1955. He worked in data processing in various positions as a wiring technician, programmer, systems analyst, project leader and programming manager. He was employed for thirteen years by the City of New York, and for sixteen years by Union Carbide. Other companies he worked for include Pandick Press, Allstate Insurance Company, and Brookhaven National Laboratory. He retired in 1998, and now lives in eastern Long Island. He has six children and twelve grandchildren.

Wil Cantey left the Army in 1954, but stayed on at the Aberdeen Proving Grounds as a Systems Analyst. In 1962, he accepted a civilian position with the Army's Strategy and Tactics Analysis Group where he worked on developing mathematical analyses of combat. In 1966, he went to work for the U.S. State Department, working in Arms Control and Disarmament, where he built probability models relating to the 18-Nation Disarmament Conferences at Geneva, Switzerland. From 1969 to 1981, he worked for the U.S. Department of Transportation. In 1981, he became the Director of Planning and Institutional Research at Howard University in Washington, DC. Sadly, on May 21, 2008, before the publication of this new edition, Wil passed away. He is survived by two children and three granddaughters.

Herb Maisel stayed in the service until 1963 as an Operations Research Analyst developing a computer simulation of land combat. He left the Department of Defense in 1963 when he was recruited by Georgetown University to establish their Computer Science Program. In 1966, he published another paper in the *Journal of the American Statistical Association*, this one titled: "The Best k of 2k – 1 Comparisons." This 16-page paper statistically analyzed sporting competitions such as the World Series in baseball, the Stanley Cup in hockey, or the NBA's playoffs, where a team must win a short series, such as four out of seven or three out of five, to advance to, or win, a championship. He has also authored or co-authored four other books (in the technology field) between 1969 and 1976. He remains a Professor Emeritus at Georgetown University and is a consultant to several organizations including the National Institute of Standards and Technology and the Commission on Professionals in Science and Technology. Herb lives in Washington, DC, with his wife, Millie. They have two sons.

Jim McDermott went to work for IBM in 1955 and worked in strategic and business planning at various IBM headquarters in Westchester County, New York. With IBM, at various times, he was the Group Director of Business Planning, Director of Market

Research, and Director of Product Forecasting. He took an early retirement in 1987 to go into independent management consulting for the technology industry. Now fully retired, he and his wife, Diane, live in Cambridge and Cape Cod. He has five children and eight grandchildren and says he doesn't miss the business world at all.

On January 2, 2008, in Las Vegas, Nevada, Roger Baldwin, Wilbert Cantey, Herbert Maisel, and James McDermott—the Four Horsemen of Aberdeen—were officially inducted into the Blackjack Hall of Fame.

ARNOLD SNYDER
BLACKJACK HALL OF FAMER

Wilbert Cantey and Herbert Maisel with
a Monroe desk calculator

THE ORIGINAL EDITION

ORIGINAL FRONT COVER

PLAYING BLACKJACK TO WIN

A New Strategy for the Game of 21

by Roger R. Baldwin, Wilbert E. Cantey
Herbert Maisel and James P. McDermott

With a foreword by
CHARLES VAN DOREN

BARROWS

Acknowledgements

We wish to thank Abraham Karp, chief of the Analytical Laboratory at Aberdeen Proving Ground, whose co-operation made our blackjack study possible.

We are grateful to Peter Ostroff and Richard Rubin for a wealth of information on the casino game.

We are likewise indebted to Howard Bainer, Robert Gessner, Otto Dykstra, Robert Pack, and John Tebbell for valuable advice and assistance.

♥ ♠ ♣ ♦

Roger R. Baldwin Wilbert E. Cantey

James P. McDermott Herbert Maisel

FOREWORD

This is a fascinating and surprising book.

It is fascinating to me because I am a bit of a mathematician and because I have more than a bit of the gambling instinct in my blood. And this book is a wonderful combination of the two — mathematics and gambling. It is good mathematics as far as I can see; and I have read the original article written by the four authors and published in the *Journal of the American Statistical Association* (it is listed among the references). Anyone with a mathematical bent would be interested, I think, to look it up. But any gambler, whether mathematically inclined or not, will recognize that *Playing Blackjack to Win* is the offspring of four young men who love to play cards, and who also love to win at playing cards. And as every gambler knows, the only thing that is more fun than gambling is winning.

But fascinating as it is, the book is even more surprising. I have been playing blackjack for more than twenty years, I guess. I have played it with my brother for matches and marbles when we were both hardly able to read the spots on the cards; I have played it at home for pennies on long winter evenings; I have played it in the army, and I have recently played a simplified version of the game with fair success on a national television program. But I find that I never really knew how to play it at all!

I suppose every player has some sort of system or other; and I would almost be willing to bet, after reading this book, that every one of those systems is wrong. I know mine was. Would you split a pair of eights, for example? Yes? No? Well then, what about

a pair of nines? Believe it or not, there is all the difference in the world between the strategies in those two
cases. (I won't say what it is — I leave it to you to find it
out.) Would you go down for double on 11? Yes? Well
then, would you on six? Would you stand on 17? Yes?
What about 12, then? Would it make any difference
what card the dealer had showing? In which version
of the game, that played in casinos in the Far West
and in the Caribbean, or that played in homes all over
the world (the so-called "home" game), do you stand
a better chance against the dealer? I would guess that
the answer to that question would fool a lot of people.
At what game, craps, roulette, or blackjack, does the
casino player stand the best chance against the house?
The answer to that one might fool you, too. Finally,
can blackjack be beaten? The answers to all these
questions, and many, many more, are in this book.

Aside from theory, there is a great deal of practical
advice. There are charts at the ends of several of the
chapters for easy reference. There is a section complete with a summary strategy chart that can be torn
out and taken to the table and, I suppose, concealed in
your hat. There is a simplified strategy for those who
play the game only for fun but who don't want to pay
too much for their recreation. There is a long chapter
on the "home" game and its psychology. There is even
a section for "sports" — that is, for players who don't
like systems; they are told, gently but firmly, that there
are certain "wild" plays that they can make without
increasing the odds against them too much, but only
certain ones. Beyond that, the authors say, beware!

In short, there is a lot in this little book; a lot of fun, and a lot of instruction. I only hope the dealers in Las Vegas don't start changing the rules to cope with the new crop of blackjack players, descending on them with copies of *Playing Blackjack to Win* sticking out of their back pockets!

CHARLES VAN DOREN
NEW YORK, N.Y.

INTRODUCTION

So you would like to win at blackjack. Fine. We can help you.

For the first time blackjack has been mathematically analyzed from top to bottom. For the first time you can learn the best play in all situations arising in a gambling casino. If you want the straight dope on when to draw or stand, when to double down, and when to split pairs, read this book!

Our strategy gives you an excellent chance of winning in any short-run period such as an evening or a weekend of casino play. While a small long-run advantage is retained by the house, it is only slightly greater than one-half of one percent! Furthermore, our strategy makes blackjack the fairest of all casino games.

Our strategy for the home game will give you a substantial edge in a group of ordinary players and enable you to hold your own even in the most experienced and crafty group.

The strategy is based on a three-year study of blackjack involving hundreds of thousands of computations on desk calculating machines. Most of the work was done in off-duty time while the authors were in the army at Aberdeen Proving Ground, Maryland. Our work is probably the most extensive mathematical analysis of any game. (This book can be read, however, by anyone who knows simple arithmetic.)

The basic mathematical theory required for this study, "the theory of probability," has been known for many decades, and, in a sense, the analysis was overdue.

A statement made in 1952 by card experts Culbertson, Morehead, and Mott-Smith[1]* emphasizes this fact.

"In no game that has been played for high stakes over so many years has there been less analysis of the science of play than in blackjack. The only available guide to strategy is empirical; no one has more than his opinion on which to estimate the advantage of the dealer."

While the theory of probability has successfully analyzed all popular *casino* games such as blackjack, craps, and roulette, it cannot handle popular *card* games such as bridge and poker. (Probability theory can compute a few interesting odds in bridge and poker. However, these odds only suggest the best play in a few situations and do not constitute a complete strategy.) Blackjack is the only popular card game within the reach of probability theory. Yet in 1953 it was the only popular casino game not yet analyzed. In a sense blackjack is "The Last of the Mohicans," and while a recently developed mathematical theory[11] eventually may analyze bridge, poker, and other popular cards games, this is not likely to happen in the foreseeable future.

---

*See pages 131–132 for all references

CHAPTER 1

The Game of Blackjack

The game of blackjack or "Twenty-One" is one of the most widely played gambling games in the world today and is the only card game regularly offered by American casinos. Its popularity transcends national boundaries and it is known under a variety of names: in England as "Van John," in Australia as "Pontoon," — both corruptions of the French "Vingt-et-un." The nomenclature may vary, but the game itself remains substantially the same.

The origins of the game have been lost in history, but it is probable that it traces back to the introduction of playing cards in Europe, some time in the fourteenth century. The game as we know it sets twenty-one as the desired total. Throughout its history, however, there have been any number of variations in this total. On Crockford's famous gambling hall in nineteenth-century London one of the more popular pastimes was "Quinze." In this variation the players attempted to get as close as possible to fifteen without exceeding that total. In order to conceal their emotions as they approached this goal the customers at Crockford's covered their faces with masks.

Another variation on the basic game, called "One-and-Thirty," was the most popular card game in both Ireland and Spain in the middle of the sixteenth century, and is still played in sections of Europe. Ireland and Spain had much contact at that time and the Irish learned the game from the Spaniards with whom it was such a fad that there was scarcely a village in Spain which had escaped its influence.

The earliest known reference to the basic game appears in Cervantes' "Comical History of Rinconete and Cortadillo," written about 1570, in which a young Spanish vagabond gives the following account of his skill at the game:

"I took along with me what I thought most necessary, and amongst the rest this pack of cards, (and now I called to mind the old saying, 'He carries his all on his back') for with these I have gained my living at all the publick houses and inns between Madrid and this place, playing at One and Thirty; and though they are dirty and torn they are of wonderful service to those who understand them for they shall never cut without leaving an ace at the bottom, which is one good point towards eleven, with which advantage, thirty-one being the game, he sweeps all the money into his pocket."

Strategies of one type or another were obviously developed to an art almost four hundred years ago.

Through the years the game of Twenty-One became a favorite of card sharks everywhere. Blackjack was one of the favorite pastimes of the Mississippi-River-boat gamblers. Indeed, most of the available early American references deal not with the nature of the game, but with its pernicious effect on the morals of youngsters. Nevertheless, it was Napoleon's favorite game and has long been one of the most popular card games among soldiers of lesser rank. The sharp practices of the past have been eliminated in the gambling casinos of today which for the most part are enjoying an unprecedented aura of respectability. The reputable gambling house need rely only on its natural "edge" to wax prosperous.

DEFINITION OF THE GAME

It should be understood at the outset that this book is primarily concerned with the presentation of a strategy of play for use in the so-called "house" game as it is played in gambling casinos throughout this country and in Cuba, Puerto Rico and other islands of the Caribbean. The primary distinction between the house game and the private game which is played at home among friends is that in the house game the dealer is a representative of the owner of the casino and, as a hired employee, must conform to a set of known rules. In the private game the deal rotates among the players, and the dealer's strategy may be dictated by a set of predetermined rules, the playing of hunches, or even the amount of beer consumed.

Obviously, in a game as fast-paced as blackjack it is imperative that the dealer have a hard-and-fast set of rules which admit of no exception. This fixed strategy imposed on the dealer is usually made public to the players. Sometimes these rules are posted prominently on the wall; sometimes they are imbedded in the surface of the table. Once in a while they are distributed in a pamphlet which also describes the game and possibly provides helpful hints on how to play. Although some slight variations on these rules exist among gambling clubs, there is a basic agreement on the main points. A best possible strategy for the house has never been computed, but through the years an accepted technique has evolved which gives the house a decided edge over the player — but not so great an edge as to overwhelm him.

Because of the subtle variation in rules among casinos, we have selected for analysis a version which, while not associated with one particular club, does consider those rules which are most common. We have prepared a strategy based on a representative game of blackjack which will be applicable in all cases regardless of variations in the rules.

THE RULES OF BLACKJACK

I. THE NUMBER OF PLAYERS

There is a dealer and from one to six players, each of whom plays solely against the dealer.

2. THE PACK

An ordinary deck of 52 cards is used.

3. THE BET

All players place their bets *before* any cards have been dealt. The club usually establishes a minimum and a maximum bet to which the players must conform. The range of these minimum and maximum bets varies widely, and usually bears a direct relationship to the type of clientele the management hopes to attract. The minimum bet is usually 50 cents to $1.00 but it is said that in Reno there are places where a bet of 10 cents is allowed.

4. THE DEAL

The players and the dealer receive two cards each, one at a time. The player receives his two cards *face down*, while the dealer gets one card face down and the other face up. If we should glance at the table at the end of the deal we would notice that the dealer's "up" card is the only one whose value can be determined at sight. Cards face down in the deal or in later play are known as "hole cards."

5. THE NUMERICAL VALUE OF THE CARDS

The numerical value of an ace may be either one or eleven at the discretion of the player. Each face card counts as ten, and all other cards retain their face value. Note that in blackjack suits make no difference. For simplicity all face cards and tens will be henceforth grouped under the general heading of "ten-value" cards. The total value of a hand is equal to the sum of the numerical values of the individual cards comprising the hand. For example:

CONTENTS OF HAND	TOTAL VALUE
Ace, 8	9 or 19
Q, 4	14
Ace, Ace	2 or 12

6. THE OBJECT OF THE GAME

The player must attempt to obtain a total in his hand which is higher than the dealer's, but which does not exceed 21.

7. NATURALS

An ace and a ten-value card (ten, jack, queen, king) when received in the deal constitute a "natural" or "blackjack." If the player has a natural and the dealer does not, then the player wins one and one-half times his original bet from the dealer. If the player does not have a natural, but the dealer does, then the player loses his original bet. If both should have a natural, then it is a tie and no money changes hands.

8. THE DRAW

After his first two cards have been dealt, the player may decide to draw no more cards. When a player makes this decision he is said to have elected to "stand." Alternatively, he may request that additional cards be dealt, face up, one at a time. Each additional card he draws is called a "hit." With each additional card received the player again has the option of standing or of drawing another card. A player continues to draw cards in this manner until he finally elects to stand, or until his total value exceeds 21 ("busts") at which point he must immediately turn up his hole cards and pay off his bet to the dealer. After each player has drawn cards in this manner, starting at the left of the dealer and proceeding in a clockwise fashion, the dealer turns up his single hole card. If his total is 16 or less, he *must* draw another card and continue drawing cards until his total reaches 17 or more at which point he must stand. If the dealer has an ace, and counting it as eleven would bring his total to 17 or more without exceeding 21, then he must consider his hand as 17 and stand.

It is important to note that this constitutes the dealer's fixed strategy. He has no choice about whether or not he should draw. His decisions are predetermined and known to the players. All of the dealer's cards are exposed at the time of the draw and there is no opportunity for bluffing or for acting contrary to the rules in any other manner. The basic rule — hit 16 and stand on 17 — is universal. Slight variations and refinements are introduced in some places, but the basic rule remains inviolate.

9. THE SETTLEMENT

If the player does not go over 21, and the dealer does, then the player wins an amount equal to his bet. If the player exceeds 21, he immediately pays the dealer the amount of his bet. Herein lies the secret of the house advantage — the player who busts must pay the house before the dealer has to draw. Only after each player has had his draw need the dealer expose his hand to the random fluctuations of Dame Chance. By this time it is not uncommon for a goodly number of the players to have already busted. Thus the house wins from those players even if the dealer should bust. If neither player nor dealer busts, the one with the higher total wins.

If neither dealer nor player busts, and both have the same total, then it is regarded as a "standoff" and no money changes hands. The practice of "ties pay the dealer" is common in many private games and greatly increases the dealer's percentage.

10. SPLITTING PAIRS

Two cards which are identical except for suit shall be defined as a pair: as, two sevens, two queens or two aces. If, before the draw, a player's hole cards form a pair, he may choose to turn them face up and treat each card as the initial card in two separate hands. This is know as "splitting pairs." The original bet is placed on one of these new hands and an equal amount is bet on the other. Then the player automatically draws one card face down on each card, and he proceeds to play with two separate hands, drawing or standing as he sees fit. The one exception to this rule concerns the splitting of aces. Because of the obvious advantage in such a move, the house rules usually state that the player may draw only *one* additional card to each ace. Furthermore, if a ten-value card should fall on one of these aces, the hand is not counted as a natural but merely as an ordinary 21 with payoff on a 1-to-1 basis if the dealer does not also get a 21. Similarly, the player who splits a pair of ten-value cards and draws an ace to one of them holds an ordinary 21. Again the payoff would only be equal to the original bet. Finally, the player is not allowed the privilege of additional splitting if, after splitting a pair, he should receive a third card of the same type forming a new pair. The dealer is not allowed to split pairs.

II. DOUBLING DOWN

After looking at his hole cards, the player may elect to double his bet and draw one additional card — no more, no less. This move is known as "doubling down." A player who elects to double down exposes his hole cards and receives his third card face down. After splitting any pair *except aces*, and after receiving an additional card on each of the split cards, the player may double down on either or both of his new hands.

12. INSURANCE BETTING

In many casinos, the player is allowed to take out an "insurance bet" whenever the dealer displays an ace as his up card. In this situation the player bets an amount of money that the dealer's hole card is a ten-value card. If it should turn out to be a ten-value card then the house pays off at the rate of 2-to-1. Thus, if you place an insurance bet exactly equal to half your original bet, you break even in the event the dealer has a natural and you don't.

For another form of insurance bet, and other casino rule variations, see Chapter 9.

CHAPTER 2

The Best Strategy for
Drawing or Standing

The first and basic problem which confronts a player during a game of blackjack is simply the question of whether to draw a card or whether to stand. This question first presents itself immediately after the deal and repeatedly thereafter, whenever the decision has been made to draw a card. It would be simplicity itself if we could approach the game with some fixed strategy similar to the dealer's. Such an accomplishment would prevent undue burdens on the brain, accelerate the rate of play, and transform the game into a card-table analogy of the slot machine — with an equivalent amount of skill necessary.

Fortunately or unfortunately, as the reader is inclined, there can be no such cut-and-dried procedure. The large edge which the house maintains allows it to follow a fixed strategy. We, in attempting to shave these odds to a minimum, must vary our strategy to fit the situation, in order to attain maximum benefit from the slight amount of information available. The one salient fact which enables us to do this is our knowledge of the dealer's automaton-like adherence to the rule, "hit 16 — stand on 17." Since the player can see one of the dealer's cards before making his first decision on drawing, he can be greatly influenced by this knowledge. For instance, if the dealer's up card were an eight we might intuitively reason that there is a very good chance that he is concealing a high card in the "hole." Therefore, we might deduce that we should seek a high total count ourselves in an attempt to beat the dealer. On the other hand, if the dealer shows a four or five, we know that his total cannot equal 17 and that he must draw another card. The odds seem to favor his "busting" in this case so we might be content to settle for a small count, such as 13 or 14, in the hope that this will happen.

Some such intuitive course of action occurs to everyone during the play, and in so doing we are mentally trying to "figure the odds" in a specific situation. For each such situation which arises there is one particular decision which the player can make which will give him the best possible chance of beating the dealer. This one decision which reduces the house percentage by the greatest amount is called the best strategy. Utilizing certain known features of probability, these best moves can be mathematically determined for each possible situation. An over-all strategy encompassing all of these possibilities will result in a mode of play which will give the greatest opportunity for beating the house.

The three basic problems in strategy are:

1. When to draw and when to stand.
2. When to double down.
3. When to split pairs.

The remainder of this chapter will consider the first of these problems.

Ordinarily a hand has a "unique" or fixed total which does not exceed 21. (Later we shall see that under certain situations a hand can have two different totals.) For each possible card which the dealer can show, there is a certain total value beyond which the player should not proceed, and up to which he should continue to draw.

The rules which the player should follow are:

1. When the dealer displays a *two* or *three* as his up card, stop on a total of *13*.

2. When the dealer's up card is a *four*, or *five* or a *six*, stop at *12*.

3. When the dealer's up card is a *seven* or higher (including an ace) stop on *17*.

These basic rules of strategy are illustrated in the chart at the end of the chapter.

To show the use of this set of rules, a simple example will serve. If the dealer shows a two after the deal, then the player should stand if his two-card total is 13 or greater. If his total is less than 13, he should continue drawing cards until the total reaches 13 or more, at which point he should stand.

These stopping points may seem surprisingly low, but an after-the-fact intuitive approach may point up the reasons. The dealer is in his weakest position when he shows a four or five or six. In fact, the possibility that he will bust is almost twice as great when his up card is six or less as when it is greater than six. There is a strong possibility that his hole card is a high-value card and that therefore his two-card total is in the vicinity of 14 or 15. Thus, according to the house rules he must draw another card, with the possibility that he will exceed 21. In this case the strategy advises that the best move is no move at all. Rather than try to beat the dealer, we should lie low and let him force himself out of the game.

Similar reasoning applies when the dealer shows a two or a three. When he displays a card greater than seven, however, it means that he may have a relative strong hand after two cards. Therefore it behooves the player in this instance to meet the dealer on his own ground and go for the high total, as is evidenced by the high stopping point.

The discussion above is admittedly after-the-fact intuition. This type of argument may not satisfy the experienced player who seriously doubts our strategy recommendations. While the mathematical proof that the recommendations are correct is not given in this book, the skeptical reader can find it in reference 10.

SOFT HANDS

At times the player will hold a hand which has two possible totals, neither of which exceeds 21. This occurs when an ace is one of the two cards. For example, a hand containing a five and an ace can, at the discretion of the player, have a total value of either 6 or 16 because the ace can be counted as a one or as an eleven. This ambiguous type of hand is known as a "soft" hand as opposed to a "unique" hand and requires special strategic considerations.

In particular: When the dealer shows a nine or a ten-value card the stopping point is 19. In all other cases the stopping point is 18. The following table summarizes the strategy for soft hands with cross marks indicating stopping points:

Player's Total	Dealer's Face-Up Card									
(soft)	2	3	4	5	6	7	8	9	10	Ace
19								X	X	
18	X	X	X	X	X	X	X			X

From this table we note that with a soft hand we should not under any circumstance stop until our total is at least 18. The player should continue to draw to his soft hand and stop at the designated stop numbers depending on the dealer's up card. If, however, the draw puts the player over 21 (and this may happen fairly often since such a high total is being hit) he should stop counting the ace as an eleven and start counting it as a one. At this point he should revert to the regular strategy for unique hands since he has but one possible total. If, for example with the dealer showing a three, a player draws a seven to a soft 15, his total will be 22. Therefore he should count the ace as one, the total becomes 12, and since the minimum stop number in this case is 13, he should draw another card.

Soft hands are valuable because with proper utilization, the player gets two chances — the first try for a high total, and if that fails there is retrenchment to a more conservative strategy.

The most surprising aspect of the optimum strategy for unique hands is the low point-total with which the player should stand when the dealer's up card is a six or less. Past analyses of the game, based in large measure on an intuitive approach and a "feel for the odds" have rarely recommended standing on a total of 13. Standing on 12 has previously been regarded as out of the question. Culbertson, Morehead, and Mott-Smith,[1] for example, recommend stopping on 14 when the situation is as above, and standing on 16 when the dealer's up card is seven or better. The strategy developed for soft hands is not quite so surprising since it is somewhat similar to that proposed by most leading authorities on the game.

The basic strategy for drawing and standing was developed in the spring of 1954. Since that time it has become second nature to us and it is difficult to recapture our original amazement. And amazement it was, since none of the established authors had provided any signposts in the proper direction. It was this initial astonishment at the low point-totals for standing which provided the impetus for the additional investigation of doubling down and splitting pairs. Little did we know the amount of computing which this further study would entail. In the study of splitting pairs, each combination of player's pair and dealer's up card required two to three hours of computing time. And there were over one hundred of these combinations. Similarly, in the study of doubling down over fifty combinations of a player's total and dealer's up card were investigated again at two to three hours per combination. The only thing which got us through this computational jungle was the long chain of surprises in the undergrowth.

Before we leave this exposition of basic strategy a brief word on insurance betting. As a general rule we do not recommend this bet. Since the insurance bet pays 2 to 1, the player must win at least one-third of the time to make the bet worthwhile. The reader will recall that the player wins the bet whenever the dealer has a ten-value card in the hole. However, since the deck contains sixteen ten-value cards, even if the player "takes out insurance" only when he has no ten-value cards in the hole, he will win only $16/49 = 32.7\%$ of his bets in the long run. The insurance bet becomes worthwhile occasionally for an expert player who can keep track of cards dealt in previous hands. This expert will notice that sometimes more than one-third of the undealt cards are ten-value cards. In such a situation the insurance bet should be placed.

THE BEST STRATEGY FOR

DEALER'S UP-CARD

The player should stand in those situations marked by the stop signal (a raised hand), and draw another card on the go signal. For example, when the dealer's face-up card is an ace, the player's strategy is described in the extreme right-hand column. This column indicates, among other things, that if the player holds a nine and six or other cards totalling 15, he should draw another card. Furthermore, the column shows that if the player subsequently draws a two—obtaining 17—he should stand.

 This symbol means STAND

 This symbol means DRAW

PLAYER'S TOTAL	2	3	4
21	STAND	STAND	STAND
20	STAND	STAND	STAND
19	STAND	STAND	STAND
18	STAND	STAND	STAND
17	STAND	STAND	STAND
16	STAND	STAND	STAND
15	STAND	STAND	STAND
14	STAND	STAND	STAND
13	STAND	STAND	STAND
12	GO	GO	STAND
11 or less	GO	GO	GO

DRAWING AND STANDING

5	6	7	8	9	10 JQK	A	
✋	✋	✋	✋	✋	✋	✋	21
✋	✋	✋	✋	✋	✋	✋	20
✋	✋	✋	✋	✋	✋	✋	19
✋	✋	✋	✋	✋	✋	✋	18
✋	✋	✋	✋	✋	✋	✋	17
✋	✋	GO	GO	GO	GO	GO	16
✋	✋	GO	GO	GO	GO	GO	15
✋	✋	GO	GO	GO	GO	GO	14
✋	✋	GO	GO	GO	GO	GO	13
✋	✋	GO	GO	GO	GO	GO	12
GO	GO	GO	GO	GO	GO	GO	11 or less
5	6	7	8	9	10 JQK	A	

CHAPTER 3

The Best Strategy for Doubling Down

Probably the most underrated and neglected aspect of play in blackjack is the technique of doubling down. Obviously many occasions arise when inspection of the two hole cards makes the player wish that he had bet more because of the advantageous situation he finds himself in. The greater our chances of victory the larger we prefer the stakes. Even the player who has bet the maximum allowed by the house often wishes he could increase that amount. The doubling-down rule presents the opportunity to do just that. Unfortunately, most players pass it by. The use of this facet of play can be a very powerful tool in shaving the house percentage to a minimum. In fact, the art of doubling down at the proper time is considered to be an integral part of the best strategy.

The best strategy for unique hands for doubling down is as follows:

1. Never double down when your two-card total is 4–8 or 12–20.

2. Double down on a total of 11 when the dealer's up card is anything but an ace.

3. Double down on a total of 10 when the dealer's up card is anything but a ten-value card or an ace.

4. Double down on a total of 9 when the dealer's up card is a two, three, four, five, or six.

This strategy is illustrated in the chart at the end of the chapter.

Intuitively we see that one would not want to double down when the dealer shows an ace because of the general strength of his hand. When our two-card total is 10 we refrain from doubling down when the up card is a ten because the dealer may too easily reach 20. Finally, when we have a total of 9, we double down only when the dealer shows weakness, viz., any card from two to six. A special table must be considered when a two-card soft hand is to be played. The cross marks indicate when the player should double down.

Player's Soft Two-Card Total	Dealer's Face-Up Card									
	2	3	4	5	6	7	8	9	10	Ace
19 or 20										
18			X	X	X					
17		X	X	X	X					
13 to 16				X	X					
12				X						

Again we note that in certain cases, soft 19 or 20, we never double down. When the dealer shows a seven, eight, nine, ten or ace we never double down regardless of our total. In the other situations there are several variations which should be memorized individually.

Note that two-card 12 consists of two aces. The table recommends that the player double down on that total when the dealer shows a five. However, a more detailed analysis shows that in this instance it is always better to split the pair of aces.

Similarly, while it is good strategy to stand on two-card soft 18 it is still better strategy to double down.

THE BEST STRATEGY FOR DOUBLING DOWN

Dealer's Up-Card	2	3	4	5	6	7	8	9	10	ACE
12 or more										
11	◉	◉	◉	◉	◉	◉	◉	◉	◉	
10	◉	◉	◉	◉	◉	◉	◉	◉		
9	◉	◉	◉	◉	◉					
8 or less										

(PLAYER'S TOTAL)

The player should double down in those situations marked by the two stacked coins. He should *not* double down in the situations marked by an empty square. For example, if the dealer's face-up card is a ten, jack, queen, or king, the player should double down on a total of 11 only.

 This symbol means DOUBLE DOWN

The player should also double down on certain soft hands when the dealer's face-up card is a six or less. The best strategy for doubling down on these soft hands is described in the text.

These are the only two exceptions and they do not cause any conflicts in strategy. Remember that it is always better to split pairs than to double down when both situations present themselves, and it is always better to double down than to stand when there is a choice.

These rules for doubling down admittedly complicate the basic strategy. It is strongly recommended, however, that they be memorized completely in whatever manner will best serve the reader's purpose. They will eventually become habit and their use automatic. It is only by taking fullest advantage of the opportunities which the house provides that we can hope to compete with the odds.

Many experienced blackjack players will undoubtedly be surprised by the number of situations in which one should double down. Doubling down in general is not recommended by any authorities on card games whom the authors have read.

CHAPTER 4

The Best Strategy for Splitting Pairs

Another aspect of play which deserves close attention is that of splitting pairs. Since this rule allows for the playing of two hands where originally there was but one, it can be highly advantageous when employed with discretion. When wisely used this practice can substantially improve the player's position.

As in doubling down, we note that pairs should be split only in certain situations. The factor which enables the player to make a decision is, again, the value of the dealer's up card.

The rules for splitting pairs follow:

1. Always split aces and eights
2. Never split tens, fives, or fours
3. Split nines unless the dealer's up card is a seven or a ten-value card or an ace
4. Split sevens, sixes, threes, and twos unless the dealer shows an eight or higher

Note the apparent discrepancy in an otherwise systematic set of rules. We do not split nines when the dealer shows a seven. Remember that he must stop on 17, so if his hole card is a ten-value card we have him beat with two nines — so why split them? If he shows an eight we do split because a total of 18 on his part would result in a standoff. Therefore we should split the pair of nines and attempt to beat him.

The fact that splitting aces is always advocated will come as no surprise to the experienced player since this practice is widely accepted and is, in fact, the only split recommended by most experts. Other aspects of the strategy may come as more of a surprise. The splitting of eights is seldom seen in the casinos, and yet is almost as important to the over-all strategy as is the splitting of aces. The splitting of ten-value cards is not recommended, and yet this practice is not uncommon. The player who is guided by hunches will often split ten-value cards when he feels that the next two cards to be dealt are ten-value cards or aces. The detailed strategy for splitting in the other situations could never be "hunched," no matter how strong the intuition.

THE BEST STRATEGY FOR SPLITTING PAIRS

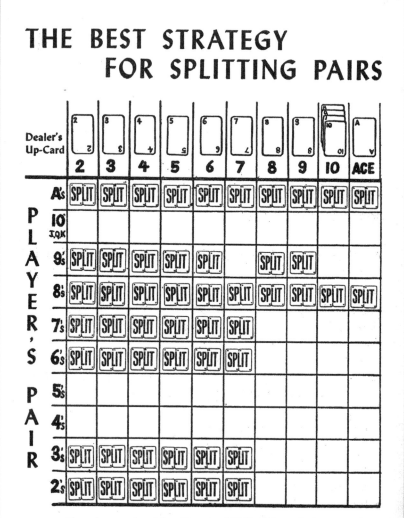

Dealer's Up-Card	2	3	4	5	6	7	8	9	10	ACE
A's	SPLIT	SPLIT	SPLIT	SPLIT	SPLIT	SPLIT	SPLIT	SPLIT	SPLIT	SPLIT
10 (J,Q,K)										
9's	SPLIT	SPLIT	SPLIT	SPLIT	SPLIT		SPLIT	SPLIT		
8's	SPLIT	SPLIT	SPLIT	SPLIT	SPLIT	SPLIT	SPLIT	SPLIT	SPLIT	SPLIT
7's	SPLIT	SPLIT	SPLIT	SPLIT	SPLIT	SPLIT				
6's	SPLIT	SPLIT	SPLIT	SPLIT	SPLIT	SPLIT				
5's										
4's										
3's	SPLIT	SPLIT	SPLIT	SPLIT	SPLIT	SPLIT				
2's	SPLIT	SPLIT	SPLIT	SPLIT	SPLIT	SPLIT				

PLAYER'S PAIR

The player should split pairs in those situations marked by the two adjacent face-up cards.

 This symbol means SPLIT THE PAIR

The player should *not* split pairs in the situations marked by an empty square. For example, if the dealer's face-up card is a two, the player's strategy is described by the extreme left-hand column. This column indicates that the player should split aces, nines, eights, sevens, sixes, threes and twos.

CHAPTER 5

Blackjack—The Fairest Game

When we first became interested in blackjack we felt that there was a real possibility that the game could be beaten. In other words, we thought that the player might be sure to win in the long run and have a better-than-even chance in any short-run period.

Our hopes were based on the fact that the dealer only has one source of advantage while the player has several. Gambling expert John Scarne[4] points up the dealer's source of advantage by recalling a deceptive sign advertising a blackjack casino: "All Ties Standoff." There is one important tie that does not result in a standoff: if both the player and dealer go over 21, the dealer wins! In compensation for this one sizable advantage of the dealer, the player has four smaller advantages:

1. Unlike the dealer, the player's strategy is not fixed by rules. For example, the player may stand on a total of 12 or draw to a total of 17, and situations exist where these plays are desirable.

2. The dealer receives one of his first two cards face up. Hence the player's strategy can take into consideration this important information about the dealer's hand. Unlike the player, the dealer cannot utilize any information about his opponents' hands.

3. The player may double down and split pairs, while these strategies are denied the dealer.

4. The player gets paid off at 1 ½ to 1 for a natural, while the dealer merely receives even money for a natural.

We had hoped that these four small advantages would overcome the one big advantage for the dealer. Well, the secret is out — the player cannot beat blackjack. However, by using the Best Strategy given in Chapters 2, 3, and 4, the player can make blackjack the fairest casino game. In other words, the blackjack player will lose less in the long run and have the best chance of winning in the short run.

The terms "short run" and "long run" have no precise definitions. We will use "long run" to mean 300,000 or more hands. This figure was selected because the player making a constant-size bet will have virtually no chance of being ahead after 300,000 hands of any casino game. "Short run" will mean 5,000 hands or less. The figure 5,000 was selected somewhat arbitrarily as the approximate number of hands of blackjack which one person could play in a week.

The house advantage in blackjack depends on the strategy used by the player. It is only .62% (or five-eighths of one percent) against the Best Strategy. This means that in the long run the house will pocket approximately .62% of the amount bet by the player. The closeness of the approximation increases with the number of hands played. For example, if the player places a $1 bet on each of one million hands, the house will almost certainly take between .32% and .92% of the amount bet, or between $3,200 and $9,200. If 100 times as many hands are played, the house will almost certainly win between .59% and .65% of the amount bet, or between $590,000 and $650,000. These examples are hypothetical, of course. It would take about five years of steady play to reach one million hands, and no player could attain one hundred million hands in a lifetime. Actually, few players ever get into the long run. Consequently, while it is interesting to know the long-run results, what happens in the short run is much more important.

A wide variety of results can occur in the short run. In particular, THE PLAYER USING THE BEST STRATEGY HAS AN EXCELLENT CHANCE OF WINNING IN THE SHORT RUN. Let us suppose, for example that the player using the Best Strategy plays one full day (900 hands), betting $1 on each hand. Suppose the results of a day's play are classified according to whether the player wins or loses $50 or more, between $25 and $50, or under $25. In the long run the percentage of days falling into each classification would be as follows:

RESULTS OF ONE DAY'S PLAY	PERCENTAGE OF DAYS
The Player Wins Over $50	3.6%
The Player Wins Between $25 and $50	12.5%
The Player Wins Less Than $25	26.8%
Total (the percentage of days the player wins)	**42.9%**
The Player Loses Less Than $25	30.7%
The Player Loses Between $25 and $50	18.9%
The Player Loses Over $50	7.5%
Total (the percentage of days the player loses)	**57.1%**
Grand Total	**100.0%**

Thus the odds that the player using the Best Strategy will not be ahead at the end of a day's play are only 4 to 3. Furthermore, the odds against substantial winnings (more than $25) are only about 5 to 1.

The house advantage against the Best Strategy in blackjack is considerably less than the house advantage in craps and roulette, the other popular American casino games. In craps the house advantage varies with the type of bet made by the player but is always at least 1.40%. Consequently, in the long run a good craps player will lose more than twice as much as the blackjack player using the Best Strategy. (We suggest that readers who are interested in the details of betting in craps see reference 5.) Usually in American roulette there are two "house numbers," zero and double-zero. The house advantage in this situation is 5.26% no matter how the player bets. Thus in the long run the roulette player will lose more than eight times as much as the blackjack player using the Best Strategy!

Furthermore, the blackjack player using the Best Strategy has a much greater chance of winning in the short run than the craps or roulette player. This fact is proved by the following table which shows the odds that the player in each of the three games will *not* be ahead at the end of 900 and 5,000 turns. The word "turn" means "action required to settle a bet" such as a hand at blackjack, a spin of the wheel at roulette, or a pass or miss-out in craps. The table assumes that the players do not vary their bets from turn to turn.

ODDS AGAINST THE PLAYER
BEING AHEAD AFTER A
CERTAIN NUMBER OF TURNS

NUMBER OF TURNS	BLACKJACK	CRAPS	ROULETTE
900	4 to 3	2 to 1	16 to 1
5,000	2 to 1	5 to 1	10,000 to 1

Note that the roulette player has almost no chance of being ahead after 5,000 turns.

Blackjack is also fairer than the popular European casino games. In European roulette only one house number exists, the zero. Furthermore, when this number comes up, the house takes only one-half the even-money bets. As a result, the house advantage against the even-money bettor is only 1.35%. (Sometimes casinos use a trickier but approximately equivalent rule for zero which is discussed in detail in reference 7.)

Two popular European games related to blackjack are baccarat-en-banque and baccarat-chemin-de-fer ("shimmy"). These games were exhaustively analyzed in 1935 by a French mathematician, George Le Myre.[8] In baccarat-en-banque the dealer's advantage against the player's best strategy is 1.11%. In baccarat-chemin-de-fer the deal passes from player to player with the casino levying a 5% tax on the dealer's winnings. The player using the best strategy for "shimmy" has a disadvantage of 1.33%. Without the casino's tax the dealer naturally would have an advantage of 1.33%. Since the dealer wins approximately one-half the time, the tax cuts his advantage by about ½ (5%) = 2 ½%, reducing it to a negative quantity. Exact calculations by Le Myre show that the casino advantage against the dealer is 1.23%.

The other popular European game is trente et quarante. We have calculated the casino advantage, and believe that it is published here for the first time: 1.10%.

The following table brings together the figures for the house advantage in the popular American and European gambling games. All figures assume that the player makes his most favorable bets and plays his best strategy.

Players all have their favorite games and many like the fast action and general razzle-dazzle of craps. Since the house advantage against a good craps player is not excessive, we do not hope to convert many craps players to blackjack. Of course, there may be some who play craps because of a mistaken belief that it offers the best odds. These players should take up blackjack.

AMERICAN GAME	EUROPEAN GAME	HOUSE ADVANTAGE	REFERENCES FOR THE FIGURES ON THE HOUSE ADVANTAGE (SEE PAGE 131)
blackjack		.62%	
	trente et quarante	1.10%	
	baccarat-en-banque	1.11%	8
	baccarat-chemin-de-fer	1.23 – 1.33%	8
	roulette	1.35%	9
craps		1.40%	5, 7
roulette		5.26%	5, 9

Roulette is another story, however. American roulette players are not given fair odds. In fact, the only thing you can say in roulette's favor is that it is fairer than horse racing! Unless a roulette player is stuck on the game or can afford to lose, we suggest he try craps or, better yet, blackjack.

CHAPTER 6

The Best Strategy in Action

The Best Strategy was recently tested in Las Vegas over a five-day period. One of the authors played 3,530 hands betting $1 per hand. While at one time he was more than $40 ahead, he ended up $26 behind. While he did not win, he certainly gave the house a good run for its money. Considering the free drinks consumed at the blackjack table, he may have broken even.

The day-by-day results are given in the following table. A minus sign in the "Winnings" column indicates a loss.

DAY	NUMBER OF HANDS PLAYED	WINNINGS
Saturday	140	$ 7.50
Sunday	790	$31.00
Monday	770	−$56.00
Tuesday	1140	−$ 4.50
Wednesday	690	−$ 4.00
Totals	3530	−$26.00

Note that we got off to an excellent start over the weekend. The roof fell in on Black Monday, however, and a slow fade took place from then on. We do not mean to imply that this pattern is general or even common. On some occasions the player will get off to a poor start and recover at the end, while on others he will start fast and quit as a winner.

The house winnings of $26 amounted to .74% of the total amount bet, $3,530. This is slightly higher than the theoretical figure of .62%. However, since only 3,530 hands were played, the actual results are not inconsistent with the theoretical figure. The above gambling results, however, do not *prove* the correctness of the .62% figure. A great many more hands must be played to obtain such an experimental proof. For example, to prove that blackjack is fairer than craps at least 200,000 hands must be played. Furthermore, a proof that the dealer's advantage against the Best Strategy is less than 1% requires over 700,000 hands. In view of these requirements for experimental proof, Las Vegas results can be considered only as preliminary evidence in our favor.

We hope to continue adding to our experimental evidence. In the meantime we must ask the reader to accept the .62% figure on a faith in the accuracy of our calculations.

Our statistical data has been supplemented by the gambling experiences of several friends. One friend, an experienced cardplayer, came off second best in blackjack for many years. By adopting the main elements of the Best Strategy, however, he recently turned the tables on the house! As of this writing, for example, he has just scored a smashing victory in Cuba, winning over one thousand dollars. Another player of our acquaintance also has used the Best Strategy to turn the tide. Formerly a consistent loser, he recently returned from a Caribbean vacation with several hundred dollars of blackjack profits.

CHAPTER 7

A Simplified Strategy for
the Casual Player

The Best Strategy described in Chapters 2, 3, and 4 is admittedly quite complicated. While the strategy is undoubtedly easier to learn than bidding in contract bridge, it requires a type of mental labor contrary to the fun-loving spirit of many cardplayers.

For the casual or occasional player, the beginner, the player who can afford to take a few extra losses, and the player not especially interested in the fine points of the game, we recommend the following "Simplified Strategy":

1. When the dealer's face-up card is a seven or higher or an ace, draw on 16 or less and stand on 17 or more. When the dealer's face-up card is a six or less, draw on 11 or less and stand on 12 or more. Count the ace as one unless counting it as eleven will make your total 18, 19, 20, or 21.

2. Always double down on 10 and 11, but never double down on any other totals.

3. Always split aces and eights, but never split any other pairs. (The poker player can remember this strategy easily by recalling that two pair, aces and eights, is the famous "dead man's hand" held by Wild Bill Hickok when he was shot and killed.)

The house advantage against the Simplified Strategy is 1.16%, or nearly double the advantage against the Best Strategy. The Simplified Strategy, however, is vastly superior to most strategies in actual use. Furthermore, the player using the Simplified Strategy still finds blackjack the fairest American casino game.

CHAPTER 8

The Price of Not Following
the Best Strategy

Departures from the Best Strategy can lead to serious losses for the player. Consider, for example, the following strategy proposed by card experts Culbertson, Morehead, and Mott-Smith in 1952:[1]

"To draw one card down to eleven is unwise. To split any pair but aces is probably unwise, and to split fours, fives, nines or tens is surely unwise. Aces should be split if the rule permits.

"When the dealer's face-up card is a seven or higher, or an ace, a count of 15 or lower should be hit; 16 or higher, stand. When the dealer's face-up card is a six or lower, except an ace, stand on 14 or more, and hit anything lower. The ace, however, should be considered as counting one unless counting it eleven will make the count 18 or better."

(The above comment does not discuss doubling down in general and opposes it specifically only for a total of 11. However, since 11 is the most favorable situation for doubling down, the advice was interpreted as opposing it in all situations.) The house advantage against this strategy is 3.62%. Since the house advantage against the Best Strategy is only .62%, a player following the advice of these experts would lose approximately *six* times as much in the long run!

The superiority of the Best Strategy will usually show itself in the short run as well. For example, the odds are greater than 3 to 1 that in one day's play (900 hands) a player using the Best Strategy will do better than a player using the Culbertson strategy. For one week's play (5,000 hands), furthermore, the odds become greater than 14 to 1. (These odds assume that both players bet the same amount and do not vary the size of their bets from hand to hand.)

Nevertheless, the Best Strategy will not always do better than other strategies in the short run. This fact can prove embarrassing. For example, you may study the Best Strategy carefully and attempt to convince a skeptical friend of its value. Your friend very likely boasts of a highly original strategy with such offbeat features as drawings on 17 and 18 and splitting fives and fours. Unfortunately, in a single day's play your skeptical friend *may* do better than you. If this happens, his skepticism runs wild, and he even may claim to have proved you wrong. Fortunately, such an exasperating turn of events is unlikely. The player should realize, however, that it *can* happen and take a patient attitude toward the results of a day's or even several days' play.

Culbertson, Morehead, and Mott-Smith are recognized authorities on card games, and their blackjack strategy is almost certainly better than most. A common strategy in the casinos, for example, involves mimicking the dealer by drawing on 16 or less, standing on 17 or more, and never splitting pairs or doubling down. The house advantage against this strategy is 5.63%. Another example is the following strategy proposed by a blackjack-playing friend with considerable casino experience: stand on any total of 12 or more, double down on 11 only, and split aces and eights only. The house advantage against this strategy is 4.25%.

Few players in the casinos like to follow a set strategy for any length of time. Impulses and hunches are usually the order of the day — and a lot of fun. A drink or two combined with the gambler's restless desire for "action" leads to many an offbeat play. The strength of the desire for action was illustrated for us in Las Vegas several years back. An exotically dressed foreign gentleman, resembling the sheik of a small but oil-rich kingdom, was playing blackjack at $20 per hand. On one occasion he received an ace and a nine for a total of 20 and drew again. He received a four, drew again, got a ten and busted. An associate asked him why he drew on 20. He replied, "You draw? You stand? It makes no difference. You've got to play!"

Impulse and hunch players undoubtedly do worse on the average than Culbertson, Morehead, and Mott-Smith. Players not familiar with the game or prone to mistakes in adding their cards are in an even weaker position. Consequently, the average house advantage considering all players is probably at least 5%.

We have seen above that the player pays a high price for choosing an over-all strategy which differs sub-stantially from the Best Strategy. It is also interesting to know the cost of specific tactics not called for by the Best Strategy.

The most serious tactical error is the failure to double down under any circumstances. The player who never doubles down but otherwise follows the Best Strategy gives the casino an additional advantage of 1.60%. The house advantage against this player is 1.60% + .62% = 2.22%, or over 3 ½ times the house advantage against the Best Strategy. As one would expect, failure to double down on a total of 11 when recommended by the Best Strategy is the most costly mistake. Failure to double down on 10 when recommended by the Best Strategy is also very serious, and 10 and 11 together account for the bulk of the loss. The following table gives the loss in failing to double down on various two-card totals in situations when doubling down is recommended by the Best Strategy.

TWO-CARD TOTAL	LOSS
11	.77%
10	.52%
9	.11%
All Soft Totals	.09%
All Totals—after splitting pairs	.11%
Total	1.60%

Clearly the player who fails to double down proceeds at his own risk!

Mistakes in strategy for drawing and standing are also costly. If the player, for example, fails to stand on 13 when the dealer's face-up card is a two or three, and fails to stand on 12 and 13 when the face-up card is a four, five, or six, but otherwise follows the Best Strategy, he loses .57%. The house advantage against this player is .57% + .62% = 1.19%, or approximately double the house advantage against the Best Strategy. If the player fails to draw on 15 and 16 when the dealer's face-up card is a seven or higher or an ace, he will lose a similar amount.

While mistakes in splitting pairs are least important, they should not be neglected. If the player always splits tens and picture cards but otherwise follows the Best Strategy, he will lose .51%. Interestingly enough, always splitting ten-value cards, a well-known policy in the casinos, is twice as costly as always splitting fives, a practically unheard-of tactic. Undesirable splitting as in the case of ten-value cards, fives, and fours, however, is less common than failure to split pairs in situations where splitting is recommended by the Best Strategy. The following table shows the price of this type of inaction.

PAIRS NOT SPLIT	LOSS
Aces	.15%
8's	.12%
9's, 7's, 6's, 3's, 2's	.17%
Total	.44%

The fact that splitting eights is almost as important as splitting aces may surprise even the most experienced players.

The relative cost of various tactical errors is illustrated by a closer look at the strategy proposed by Culbertson, Morehead, and Mott-Smith. Recall that the house advantage against their strategy is 3.62% as opposed to .62% against the Best Strategy. Thus the house advantage is increased by 3%. *Over half* of the increase is due to failure to double down under any circumstances! About one-third is due to faulty strategy for drawing and standing, while only one-tenth is from mistakes in splitting pairs. The importance of doubling down is underlined once more.

We hope this chapter has hoisted a STORM WARNING for small billfolds west of the Rockies and south of the Gulfstream: if you plan to play blackjack for any length of time, do not depart substantially from the Best Strategy! If you do choose to "go it alone," look to your reserves!

CHAPTER 9

Variations in Casino Rules

The rules described in Chapter 1 are for the casino game as played in Nevada and the Caribbean. Each casino, however, has its own rules which agree with those of other casinos on the main points but which often differ on details. As a result, the rules given in Chapter 1 are common but not universal.

This chapter discusses variations on the rules in Chapter 1. The only variations considered are those which have been either observed personally, reported in the most recent publications on card games, or described by experienced casino players of our acquaintance.

The variations encountered never require a change in the player's strategy. In other words, the Best Strategy always holds. However, they do have important effects on the house advantage.

The most dangerous variation for the player is the rule restricting doubling down to totals of 11 *only*. We have not seen this "11 only" variation anywhere in Nevada. However, several authors[2, 6] on card games refer to doubling down strictly in terms of doubling down on a total of 11. Perhaps their implication is that the casinos do not permit doubling down on other totals. Possibly, the "11 only" variation exists in a few Nevada casinos. In any case, this variation definitely holds throughout the casinos of Puerto Rico. To make matters worse, the casinos in Puerto Rico reserve the right to forbid doubling down on 11 as well! In Cuba, on the other hand, we know of no restrictions on doubling down.

The rule restricting doubling down to totals of 11 increases the house advantage by .83%. Consequently, a casino with this rule has an advantage of .83% + .62% = 1.45% against the Best Strategy, over twice the advantage under the standard rules. Furthermore, the house which does not allow any doubling down will gain 1.60%, bringing its advantage to 2.22%. We urge serious blackjack players to be on their guard against the "11 only" and "no doubling down" rules. If possible, they should avoid casinos with these rules!

Other variations in rules are less important to the player. Frequently the casinos forbid doubling down on soft hands or after splitting pairs. These rules increase the house advantage by only .09% and .11%, respectively. Sometimes the player is not allowed to split aces, a rule costing him .15%.

Another common variation requires the dealer to draw on soft 17. This rule helps the dealer when his face-up card is an ace, hurts him slightly when his face-up card is a six or less, and has no effect when his face-up card is a seven, eight, nine, ten, or picture card. (The rule has no effect in this latter situation because the dealer cannot possibly obtain soft 17 starting with those face-up cards.) The over-all increase in the dealer's advantage is .20%. A tricky version of this rule requires the dealer to hit soft 17 only when his face-up card is an ace. This hurts the player slightly more (.24%). In some casinos the dealer has the option of drawing or standing on soft 17. This option enables the clever dealer to gain somewhat more than .24%.

If all the minor variations above were in effect simultaneously, the increase in the house advantage would be .55%, a considerable amount. However, we have not seen any one casino where more than two of these variations were in effect. Furthermore, these negative variations may be offset by variations helping the player.

A common rule variation helping the player allows him to double down on any *three* cards as well as any *two*. Suppose, for example, the player's first two cards are a three and a four, and he chooses (correctly) not to double down. He draws another four for a total of 11. Under the variation, he can now double down. This variation decreases the house advantage by .19%. Interestingly enough, the variation allowing the player to double down any time, that is on *two*, *three*, and *four or more* cards, only helps him slightly more (.20%).

Sometimes the casino allows the player who splits a pair of aces to draw more than one card to each ace. This variation enables the player to treat the aces like any other split pair and cuts the house advantage by .22%.

Usually the casino allows the player to split "triplets" and "quadruplets" as well as pairs. This option arises when the player splits a pair and receives face down a third and possibly a fourth card of the same type. Thus the rules variation allows the player to play three or possibly four individual hands at the same time. Unfortunately, the variation cuts the house advantage by only .04%.

Some casinos pay bonuses for unusual hands such as three sevens or naturals formed by the ace and jack of spades.[4] These hands will win a fixed amount such as $5 providing the player's bet exceeds the minimum.

Hands resulting in bonuses are extremely rare and the player should not depart from the Best Strategy in order to play for them. Furthermore, bonuses usually have very little effect on the dealer's advantage.

In some Caribbean casinos all the players' cards are dealt face up. The dealer continues to receive one card face down and the rest face up. One might think at first that this rule gives the dealer a big advantage. However, since the dealer's strategy is fixed by house rules, he cannot make use of his complete knowledge of the players' hands. Consequently, in an honest game this rule has no effect on the Best Strategy or the house advantage. While it will help a dealer who wants to cheat, the rule is usually accompanied by a requirement that the cards be dealt from a box or "shoe." This requirement makes cheating much more difficult.

Whenever all the players' cards are dealt face up, two or more packs of cards are used. While the Best Strategy has been worked out assuming one deck, the use of two or more decks will not require any changes, except possibly in some very minor details. Furthermore, the house advantage against the Best Strategy remains the same.

The Insurance Bet can be placed in most Nevada casinos but is frequently not permitted in the Caribbean. A friend of modest means learned this the hard way. He forgot himself for the moment and slapped down a $30 bet, half of his available cash. When the dealer faced an ace, our friend lunged for his wallet, planning to make a $15 Insurance Bet. Imagine the scene: the $30 bet, the threatening ace, our friend eagerly clutching three $5 bills. The dealer was polite but oh, so suave. "Señor," he said, "we do not do that here." P.S. the dealer had a natural.

In some casinos the player is also allowed to "take out insurance" when the dealer shows a ten-value card. If the dealer has an ace in the hole, the insurance bet is paid off at 10 to 1. This bet is less favorable than the standard insurance bet and likewise is not recommended.

While the Insurance Bet is not a good gamble, it has some nongambling value. A friend sometimes takes advantage of the substantial interest and confusion centering on this bet. He has been known to start conversations with pretty girls at the blackjack tables by asking, "What's Insurance?"

This chapter probably covers most of the variations in rules. We do not pretend to know about all existing variations, however, and certainly cannot predict possible variations in the future.

This chapter has dealt exclusively with the rules in Nevada and the Caribbean. Blackjack is played in casinos in other parts of America, though frequently the game is not legal. The rules for these games may vary considerably, and we advise the player to proceed with caution.

Our discussion of the rules should also include some comments on the possibility of cheating by the dealer. All our calculations and statements have assumed that casino blackjack is an honest game. We have never seen anything to lead us to doubt this assumption.

Blackjack dealers, however, are extremely fast and skillful. They can deal nearly 100 hands an hour to each of three or four players, and, in addition, handle all cash transactions. Many of them are artists in their own way and have a motion and style as impressive as a skilled athlete or fine dancer. We have always felt that if they wanted to cheat and get away with it, they could. Only a real cardsharp could catch them.

Aside from questions of principle, however, cheating would seem to be against their basic self-interest. The house has a substantial advantage against most players and will usually take their bankroll anyhow. So why rush? Even more important, a casino has a lot to lose by becoming tainted by suspicions — let alone proof — of dishonesty.

CHAPTER 10

Using the Exposed Cards to Improve Your Chances

The casual player probably should skip this chapter. However, we suggest that the serious player study the chapter carefully. He will find information enabling him to capitalize fully on his cardplaying ability.

The Best Strategy described in Chapters 2-4 is based on (1) the dealer's face-up card, and (2) the player's total. This chapter shows how to use a third item of information: the cards previously dealt. Proper use of this information enables the player to make certain improvements on the Best Strategy.

The reader may be puzzled by the statement that improvements can be made in the Best Strategy. Strictly speaking, however, the Best Strategy is the best of all the strategies which use only the first two items of information above. While it is better than most intuitive strategies which use information on the cards previously dealt, this superiority cannot be guaranteed. Furthermore, some strategies which use knowledge of the "out cards" are superior to the Best Strategy. One of these is presented in this chapter.

Any discussion of modifying the Best Strategy must begin with the elementary fact that a full deck contains four cards in each of the thirteen ranks (4 aces, 4 kings, 4 queens, etc.). Since there are 52 cards altogether, the proportion of each rank in a full deck is $4/52 = 1/13$. As the deal progresses, however, the composition of the undealt cards becomes different from the full-deck composition. For example, when half the deck has been dealt, the proportion of any particular rank may range from 0 to $4/26 = 2/13$. Furthermore, unless exactly two cards in the rank remain, the full-deck proportion has changed.

The composition of the undealt cards directly affects the odds on the cards drawn by the player and dealer. A change in these odds, furthermore, will frequently alter the player's best play. In particular, since the Best Strategy assumes a full-deck composition at all times, compositions of the undealt cards which differ substantially from the full deck will require changes in the Best Strategy. For example, if all ten-value cards, nines, and eights have been dealt, the player should draw on 12, 13, and 14 even when the dealer's face-up card is a four, five, or six. (Recall that the Best Strategy recommends standing on 12 or more for these face-up cards.) Similarly, if only ten-value cards remain in the deck, the player must stand on a total of 12 even when the dealer's face-up card is a seven or higher, or an ace. (Recall that the Best Strategy recommends drawing on 16 or less in this situation.) Fortunately, the changes in the Best Strategy required by non-full-deck compositions rarely will be as great as in the above examples.

The reader may be disturbed, however, by the fact that the Best Strategy can be wrong. A friend, for example, was astonished to hear that our strategy ignored the cards previously dealt, and, as a consequence, lapsed into occasional errors. The reader can be assured, nevertheless, that in the majority of situations the Best Strategy will be correct. Furthermore, the Best Strategy's errors are already taken into account in the .62% figure for the dealer's advantage. In other words, the player can relax, ignore the cards previously dealt, make these occasional errors, and still hold down the dealer's advantage to .62%.

Since the composition of the full deck is known, keeping track of all the cards which have been dealt automatically shows the composition of the undealt cards. Unfortunately, keeping track of all the cards previously dealt, or, as gamblers say, "casing the cards," is extremely difficult. It is probably tougher, for example, than remembering all the cards played at contract bridge. While the card-caser can disregard the suits of the cards in blackjack, he must acquire his information at a much faster rate than in bridge. There is no doubt that card-casing requires unusual natural ability plus considerable practice.

Most players, including many serious blackjack players, will not want to case the cards. It is too tough, too much work, and generally takes the fun out of the game. Consequently, this chapter presents a system of "partial casing" requiring the player to notice only a few cards. Furthermore, no memory work is needed.

In most casinos the player receives his first two cards face down during the *deal*, and all others face up during the *draw*. *Our system requires the player to sit at the dealer's right and keep track of the cards drawn by the other players during the present hand. The system also requires a thorough command of the Best Strategy.* All this should not be difficult for most players. In the first place, the seat at the dealer's right is surprisingly easy to get. Secondly, many players already make a habit of keeping track of the cards drawn in the present hand. Finally, the Best Strategy is not unduly difficult to memorize thoroughly, certainly no more difficult than a bidding system in contract bridge.

When the player is on the dealer's right and four or five other players are at the table, usually at least three cards will be drawn by the other players. The player following the partial-casing system uses this information plus the knowledge of his own hole cards.

To simplify the statement of the partial-casing system let us define the term "player's (or dealer's) minimum satisfactory total" as the smallest total on which the player (or dealer) will stand. For example, the dealer's minimum satisfactory total is always 17. As another example, when the dealer's face-up card is a two, the Best Strategy requires the player to draw on 12 or less and stand on 13 or more. Consequently, in this case the player's minimum satisfactory total is 13.

If the last few cards drawn are all ten-value cards, the chance for another ten-value card is reduced, and the player will be encouraged to draw. On the other hand, if the last few cards drawn are all low cards (aces, twos, threes, fours, and fives), the chance for another low card is reduced, and the player will be encouraged to stand. The exact number of consecutive ten-value or low cards required to change the Best Strategy is a difficult mathematical problem demanding extensive analysis. We will not bore the reader with mathematical details, however, and merely state the basic conclusions.

1. When the dealer's face-up card is a six or less and the last 3 cards drawn are ten-value cards, the Best Strategy's minimum satisfactory totals should be raised by 1. In other words, when the dealer's face-up card is a two or three, the player should draw now on 13 or less and stand on 14 or more; and when the

dealer's face-up card is a four, five, or six, the player should draw now on 12 or less and stand on 13 or more. If the last 5 cards drawn are ten-value cards, the Best Strategy's minimum satisfactory totals should be raised by 2.

If the player has a ten-value card in the hole, the requirements for 3 and 5 consecutive ten-value cards are reduced to 2 and 4, respectively. The player probably will find it easier, however, to memorize the 3 and 5 requirements and count any ten-value card in the hole as part of the sequence of ten-value cards drawn.

2. When the dealer's face-up card is a seven, eight, nine, or ten-value card and the last 4 cards drawn are low (aces, twos, threes, fours, or fives), the Best Strategy's minimum satisfactory totals should be lowered by *one*. In other words, the player now should draw on 15 or less and stand on 16 or more. Furthermore, when the dealer's face-up card is a seven or eight and the last 7 cards drawn are low, the Best Strategy's minimum satisfactory totals should be lowered by *two*. When the dealer's face-up card is a nine or ten-value card, the player should forget about the 7 requirements and never lower the Best Strategy's minimum satisfactory totals by more than *one*.

If the player has a low card in the hole, the requirements for 4 and 7 consecutive low cards are reduced to 3 and 6, respectively. Two low cards in the hole reduce these requirements to 2 and 5, respectively. Again the player probably will find it easier to memorize the 4 and 7 requirements and count low cards in the hole as part of the sequence of low cards drawn.

3. When the dealer's face-up card is an ace, the Best Strategy should never be changed. In other words, the player should always draw on 16 or less and stand on 17 or more.

4. Even when a long sequence of ten-value cards are drawn, the player should never draw on 17. (All four rules above apply to unique totals only, and the player should always draw on soft 17).

The four basic rules are summarized by the following chart of the player's minimum satisfactory totals.

DEALER'S FACE-UP CARD

Player's Total	2	3	4	5	6	7	8	9	10	Ace	Player's Total
18-21											18-21
17						B-S	B-S	B-S	B-S	B-S	17
16						4L	4L	4L	4L		16
15	5T	5T				7L	7L				15
14	3T	3T	5T	5T	5T						14
13	B-S	B-S	3T	3T	3T						13
12			B-S	B-S	B-S						12
11											11
or less											or less

Explanation of the symbols in the chart:
  B-S – The minimum satisfactory totals (MSTs) recommended by the Best Strategy.
  3T – The MSTs recommended when the last 3 cards drawn are ten-value cards.
  5T – The MSTs recommended when the last 5 cards drawn are ten-value cards.
  4L – The MSTs recommended when the last 4 cards drawn are low.
  7L – The MSTs recommended when the last 7 cards drawn are low.

The four basic rules apply to casinos using one deck of cards. When two decks are used, twice as many consecutive ten-value cards or low cards must be drawn to make the same changes in the minimum satisfactory totals. For example, when the dealer's face-up card is a six or less, 6 consecutive ten-value cards must be drawn to raise the minimum satisfactory totals by *one* instead of 3 as in rule (1) above. For this reason, the partial-casing system is considerably less effective in casinos using two or more decks.

The player should always consider his own draw as part of the sequence of cards drawn. For example, suppose the dealer's face-up card is a two and the player's hole cards are a two and an ace, totaling soft 13. Suppose the player draws a ten-value card, obtaining unique 13. When the dealer's face-up card is a two, the Best Strategy's minimum satisfactory total is 13, indicating the player should stand. However, if the 2 cards drawn before the player's draw are ten-value cards, the player must count his own draw and consider that 3 consecutive ten-value cards have been drawn. The player should then follow rule (1) above and draw on 13.

If the player is not able to observe a sufficient number of draws, no changes should be made in the Best Strategy. For example, suppose the dealer's face-up cards is a six or less, the player has no ten-value cards in the hole, and only 2 cards have been drawn. Even if both these cards are ten-value cards, the Best Strategy should not be changed.

The partial-casing system applies only to the player's strategy for drawing and standing on unique totals.

However, the strategy for soft hands also has been studied mathematically. The basic conclusion is that the Best Strategy should not be changed. The one exception is when the dealer's face-up card is an ace and the last 3 cards drawn are ten-value cards. In this case the Best Strategy's minimum satisfactory total should be raised by one. In other words, the player should draw on soft totals of 18 or less and stand on soft totals of 19 or more.

No mathematical analysis has been attempted on a partial-casing system which changes the Best Strategy for doubling down and splitting pairs. The work involved in such a study would require a Hercules, or better yet, an IBM computer. In the absence of a definite method for changing the Best Strategy, we suggest that no changes be made. Ill-considered changes probably will do more harm than good.

Likewise, we do not know exactly how much the partial-casing system cuts the dealer's advantage. In our opinion, however, the cut is certainly less than 1% and probably less than ½%. As a result, there is no guarantee that partial casing will overcome the dealer's .62% advantage. Nevertheless, a gain of even .3% cuts the dealer's advantage in half and should not be neglected.

Most experienced players should be able to adopt the system of partial-casing without much difficulty. Many of these players already make a habit of adjusting their strategy according to the cards showing on the table. However, these adjustments are made generally on the basis of guesswork and intuition. The four rules in this chapter give the player a more precise and effective means of using this information.

Many players overemphasize the results of the last few draws, and, as a result, make drastic and costly changes in their strategy. For example, when four consecutive low cards are drawn, these players feel that the fifth card almost certainly will *not* be low. As a result, they may stand on 14 or 15 when the dealer's face-up card is a seven or higher. Actually, a sequence of four consecutive low cards only *reduces* the probability that the fifth card is low. Furthermore, this probability often is decreased by as little as 20%. Consequently, standing on 16 or more is the best play in this situation, while standing on 14 or 15 is a costly mistake.

When the dealer's face-up card is a seven or higher, the Best Strategy recommends drawing on 16 or less and standing on 17 or more. In the above example the player who was willing to stand on 14 or 15 would have been better off sticking strictly to the Best Strategy. The example is typical! A player who jumps to conclusions on the basis of the last few draws usually does worse than the player who ignores this information altogether and follows the Best Strategy.

The partial-casing system guards against this common tendency to overemphasize the last few draws. It rarely leads to changes of more than 1 in the Best Strategy's minimum satisfactory totals. At least four consecutive ten-value cards are required for a raise of 2, and at least five consecutive low cards are required for a drop of 2. The odds against each of these sequences are greater than 100 to 1.

CHAPTER 11

A Special Word to "The Sport"

Many players do not like to follow systems. They get their kicks from experiments and adventures at the gambling tables. Since their enjoyment of variety in the play is often stronger than their desire to win, these players might be known as "sports."

There is an old gambler's saying, "A player without a system is seldom without a dollar." Rumor has it that the saying originated with an old-time sport who once in his lifetime tried a system and lost heavily.

Very often the sport is a free-wheeling spender who glorifies in the big bet as well as the bold move. In blackjack he is truly in his element when making the largest bet at the table and subsequently splitting a pair or doubling down. He also likes to draw recklessly and push his luck generally.

While we are basically system players, there is a little of the sport in each of us. Therefore, we are happy to suggest some optional plays for the sport. While these are losing plays in the long run, he will not lose much and should get a kick out of the extra action.

THE SPORT'S OPTIONS

1. DOUBLING DOWN

The sport probably will want to double down whenever this play is recommended by the Best Strategy. The sport also may double down on 11 when the dealer's face-up card is an ace; on 10 when the dealer's face-up card is an ace or ten-value card; on 9 when the dealer's face-up card is a seven; and on 8 when the dealer's face-up card is a five or six. In addition, the sport has the option of doubling down on soft 19 when the dealer's face-up card is a four, five, or six; on soft 18 when the dealer's face-up card is a two or three; on soft 17 when the dealer's face-up card is a two; and on soft 13 through soft 16, inclusive, when the dealer's face-up card is a four.

2. SPLITTING PAIRS

The sport probably will want to split pairs whenever this play is recommended by the Best Strategy. The sport also may split nines when the dealer's face-up card is a seven or ten-value card; split sevens, sixes, threes, and twos when the dealer's face-up card is an eight; and split fours when the dealer's face-up is a five or six. Even the sport should not split ten-value cards.

3. DRAWING AND STANDING

When the dealer's face-up card is a six or less and the sport has a hunch that a ten-value card is not forthcoming, he should raise the Best Strategy's minimum satisfactory totals by 1. In other words, when the dealer's face-up card is a two or three, he should draw on 13 or less and stand on 14 or more; and when the dealer's face-up card is a four, five, or six, he should draw on 12 or less and stand on 13 or more. Otherwise, the sport should follow the Best Strategy.

The above adventures should be well within the means of any fun-loving sport. However, he should be prepared to pay extra for the privilege of further experimentation.

CHAPTER 12

The Home Game

The home or "private" game of blackjack is played throughout the United States and traditionally rivals poker as the most popular game in the Armed Forces. The home game is simple to learn and a lot of fun to play. Only two players are needed to get up a game, though four to six probably make the best game. Play is fast and all hands are played to a showdown. (The player never drops out in the early stages of a hand as frequently happens in poker.) Unlike the casino game, the dealer can stand or draw on any total. The flexibility of the dealer's strategy introduces bluffing and other fascinating elements into the home game. The rotation of the deal adds zest by giving each individual two different strategic roles.

The Stakes

In a friendly game the stakes are high enough to be interesting but not high enough to hurt anyone seriously. Attention can be focused on the play of individual hands without excessive worry over the financial results of the evening. Even the losers can enjoy themselves — a little.

In a friendly game the minimum bet is low enough to be within the financial reach of all the players. In many games a dime or quarter minimum is not considered too low. Since the greatest liability lies with the dealer, he is usually allowed to set the maximum bet subject only to very broad limitations. For example, if the minimum bet is a dime or quarter, the dealer might be allowed to choose any maximum from a half dollar on up. Sometimes he is allowed to call "The sky's the limit!" The dealer is always allowed to sell the deal or give it away at any time. This enables any player "with the shorts" to avoid the greater risks of the deal.

If play begins in the early evening, the game often thins out sometime after midnight. The casual players and small-money men retire, leaving the "sharks" to thrash around. At this stage the minimum and maximum bets are usually increased by mutual consent.

Sometimes the stakes are increased from game to game. While this "creeping inflation" in the stakes adds excitement to the play, it also creates problems. Differences of opinion often develop on the proper stakes, and disputes arise between "hard-money" and "big-money" factions. Some players may lose more than they can afford and drop out of the game. In the extreme case, the friendly game becomes a tough game or break up altogether.

RULES FOR THE HOME GAME

There are many variations to the home game, considerably more than in the casino game. We have compiled a list of common variations by talking with over forty home-players in Maryland, New York, and South Carolina. It is not possible to say that there is one "standard" game which is more popular than any other. Therefore, the following rules define a version of the game which is common but by no means universal. The important variations are indicated. (Note: the rules governing the pack, the numerical value of the cards, and the object of the player are the same as for the casino game. See Chapter 1.)

1. NUMBER OF PLAYERS
Two to fourteen.

2. BETTING
The players make their bets before any cards are dealt. (Variation: the player looks at his first card before placing his bet. Sometimes in this variation the dealer may also look at his first card and has the option of doubling all the players' bets. When the dealer doubles all bets, each player has the option to redouble.)

3. THE DEAL
The players and dealer each receive two cards, one face up and one face down. (Variation: each player gets both cards face down.)

4. NATURALS
If a player has a natural and dealer does not, the player receives twice his original bet from the dealer. If a player does not have a natural and the dealer does, the player loses his original bet. If both player and dealer have naturals, no money changes hands. (Variation: the player loses his original bet.) If the dealer's face-up card is an ace or ten-value card, he must immediately look at his hole card. If he has a natural, he collects at once, and the hand is terminated prior to the draw. (Variation: sometimes an ace and a ten counts as ordinary 21 only.)

5. THE DRAW
The rules are the same as for the casino game except that the dealer is not required to draw or stand on any particular totals. (Variation: the dealer must draw on totals of 16 or less and stand on totals of 17 or more.)

6. BONUSES

If the first *five* cards dealt to the player total 21 or less, he receives twice his original bet from the dealer. If his first *six* cards total 21 or less, he receives three times his original bet (variations: two, four, five, and six times). These bonuses are paid regardless of the dealer's hand. Note, however, that a dealer's natural would be shown prior to the draw and the player would not have the opportunity of drawing for these bonuses. The dealer never receives any bonuses.

7. THE SETTLEMENT

The rules are the same as for the casino game except that if neither player nor dealer busts and both have the same total, the dealer wins. (Variation: no money changes hands.)

8. SPLITTING PAIRS

The rules are the same as for the casino game except that the player who splits aces may draw as many cards as he likes to each ace. (Variation: the player is not allowed to split aces. Variation: a ten-value card falling on a split ace and an ace falling on a split ten-value card constitute a natural.)

9. DOUBLING DOWN

The rules are the same as for the casino game except the player is not permitted to double down on totals other than 11. (Variation: the player may double down on any two cards.)

10. CHANGING THE DEAL

To start the game the pack is shuffled and cut, and the cards are dealt in rotation face up until a jack of clubs or spades is turned up. The player receiving the "black jack" becomes the first dealer. He continues to deal until another player has a natural. The player with the natural becomes the next dealer. If more than one player has a natural, the player nearest the dealer's left receives the deal. If both player and dealer have naturals, the deal does not shift. Between hands the dealer may sell the deal or give it away at any time. In the event that no player will buy or accept the deal, the next dealer is selected by the "black jack" method used at the beginning of the game. (Variation: sometimes the deal shifts after a fixed number of deals.)

II. IRREGULARITIES
(Discussed in the Appendix, pages 129 and 130.)

Editorial Comments on the Rules. In our opinion the game is improved if the player is allowed to split any pair and double down on any two cards. This simplifies the rules, allows the player some interesting additional options, and tends to cut down on the dealer's advantage.

GENERAL PRINCIPLES FOR THE PLAYER
All the strategy recommendations in this chapter are based on the "standard" home game defined by the above rules. Where possible the changes in strategy required by variations in rules also will be indicated.

In the casino game the player's strategy was based on two items of information: (1) the dealer's face-up card, and (2) the player's total. In the home game a third item must be considered: the dealer's strategy for drawing and standing. The player must make some type of reasonable prediction concerning the future action of the dealer. Predicting the dealer's strategy is difficult and requires considerable card sense, experience, and psychological skill. This additional problem, however, makes the home game more complicated and in a sense more challenging than the casino game.

We would like to suggest four basic principles for predicting the dealer's strategy and making use of these predictions.

Principle 1:
⇒ **Study the dealer's general playing habits**
Some dealers are not hard to figure. They play strictly according to a system such as "draw on 16 or less, stand on 17 or more." In particular, the player should learn to distinguish four main dealer's strategies: (1) the *supercautious* strategy — always stand on 15 or more; (2) the *cautious* strategy — always draw on 15 or less and stand on 16 or more; (3) the *casino* strategy — always draw on 16 or less and stand on 17 or more; and (4) the *bold* strategy — always draw on 17 or less. Many dealers vary their strategy but lean strongly toward systems such as the above. The player who studies the dealer can often discover these inclinations.

Principle 2:
⇒ **When in doubt about the dealer's general playing habits, assume that he follows the casino strategy**
Drawing on 16 or less and standing on 17 or more is probably the most common of the four strategies described above. Many dealers feel that since the casino dealers follow this strategy, it must be good.

<u>Principle 3</u>:
⇒ Study the players' bets and face-up cards for clues on whether the dealer will depart from his general playing habits

The dealer's right is the best position for making such a study. The player on the dealer's left has much less information but can at least notice the appearance of his own hand.

The player should observe the size of the bets and the values of the players' face-up cards. (He also should notice his own bet and face-up cards.) He should examine this information from the dealer's point of view. For example, if a big bettor (or a majority of the players) can be figured for 18 or more, the dealer probably will become more daring. If his natural inclination is to be cautious, he now may follow the casino strategy; while if he normally follows the casino strategy, he may become bold. On the other hand, a big bettor may stand pat on his first two cards with a five showing. Since players almost always draw on an ace and a five (soft 16), he can be figured for 15 or less. Consequently, the dealer very likely will become less daring.

If, as in the above example, the player stands pat with hole card(s) totaling at most six, he has what we will call "an exposed low hand." His total cannot possibly exceed 17. Furthermore, since most players draw on soft 17, he almost certainly has 16 or less. If two or more exposed low hands appear at the table, the dealer invariably will become less daring. If one exposed low hand appears at the table, the dealer may become less daring depending on other factors such as the bets and face-up cards of the other players.

In a common variation of the home game the players receive both cards face down. This rule makes it very difficult for the dealer to figure the players' hands, and he is practically forced to fall back on a general strategy such as the casino strategy or the cautious strategy. In this situation the information in the present hand is not very important for predicting the dealer's strategy, and the player should concentrate on studying the dealer's general playing habits.

Principle 4:
⇒ The more the dealer draws, the more the player should stand

The reasons for this are easy to understand. The player can win in two ways: (1) "the hard way" — by obtaining a total which is greater than the dealer's but which does not exceed 21, and (2) "the easy way" — by obtaining a total which does not exceed 21 when the dealer busts. The more the dealer draws, the more likely he will go over 21. Therefore, it becomes less difficult to beat him "the easy way." Similarly, the more the dealer draws, the greater will be his final total if he does not bust. Thus it will be more difficult to beat him "the hard way." Consequently, the more the dealer draws, the more the player should attempt to beat him "the easy way" — by standing.

The above four principles are admittedly very general. However, specific techniques for applying them are described in the following sections.

The Player's Drawing Strategy When the Dealer's Face-up Card is a Two, Three, Four, or Five

In this situation the dealer rarely will stand pat on his first two cards. Furthermore, because of the large number of ten-value cards in the deck, there is an excellent chance that his first two cards total between 12 and 15. Since the dealer almost always draws on such totals, there is a good chance he will go over 21.

For These Face-up Cards the Player Usually Should Stand on Any Total of 12 or More

While this strategy may surprise many readers, it is very similar to the strategy for the casino game. The strategy follows from the basic fact that there is an excellent chance the dealer will bust. Therefore, the player, like Br'er Rabbit, should lie low.

There are some exceptions to this rule. If the dealer follows the cautious strategy, the player should draw on 12 and 13 but stand on 14 or more. Furthermore, in the exceptional case where the dealer follows the supercautious strategy, the player should draw on 15 or less and stand on 16 or more.

Exposed low hands may be treated as exceptions. If the dealer generally follows the casino strategy, an exposed low hand may lead him to adopt the cautious strategy. Consequently, the player usually should draw on exposed low hands which total 12 or 13, such as a five showing and a seven or eight in the hole.

The Player's Drawing Strategy When the Dealer's Face-up Card is a Six

In this situation the player is on the horns of a dilemma and must lean very heavily on his prediction of the dealer's strategy. The player should act as if the dealer has a ten-value card in the hole, giving him 16. If the player predicts the dealer will stand on 16, he should draw on 16 or less and stand on 17 or more. On the other hand, if the player feels the dealer will draw on 16, he should stand on any total of 12 or more. If the player has an exposed low hand, he may figure that the dealer will stand on 16. In this situation he should draw on his exposed low hand unless he has an ace in the hole.

While the player's strategy seems to assume that the dealer *always* has a ten-value card in the hole, this assumption is used only to simplify the explanation and memorization of the strategy. Actually, the strategy is based on detailed mathematical calculations which assume that the chance the dealer has a ten-value card in the hole is 16 in 51.

The Player's Drawing Strategy When the Dealer's Face-up Card is a Seven, Eight, or Ace

In this situation the dealer often will stand pat on his first two cards. If his face-up card is a seven or eight, the large number of ten-value cards in the deck give him a good chance of holding 17 or 18. If his face-up card is an ace, he has a good chance of holding some total between 17 and 20. Consequently, the chances are not good that the dealer will bust. (This is particularly true when his face-up card is an ace.) Furthermore, totals of 17 and 18 are *not* extremely difficult to beat by drawing.

For These Face-up Cards the Player Usually Should Draw on 16 or Less and Stand on 17 or More

In other words, when the dealer shows a seven, eight, or ace, the player should meet him on his own ground. The only exception to this rule is when the dealer follows the bold strategy. In this case the player should stand on any total of 12 or more.

The Player's Drawing Strategy When the Dealer's Face-up Card is a Nine or Ten-Value Card

In this situation the dealer often will stand pat on his first two cards and has a good chance of holding 19 or 20. The chances are not good that the dealer will bust. On the other hand, totals of 19 and 20 *are* extremely difficult to beat by drawing. Consequently, the player should draw less than when the dealer's face-up card is a seven, eight, or ace.

For These Face-up Cards the Player Usually Should Draw on 14 or Less and Stand on 15 or More

However, if the player has an exposed low hand or for any other reason predicts the dealer will follow a cautious or supercautious strategy, he should also draw on 15 and 16. On the other hand, if the player feels the dealer will follow a bold strategy, he should stand on any total of 12 or more.

Summary of the Player's Drawing Strategy

The entries in the following table give the recommendations for the player's strategy.

DEALER'S STRATEGY

DEALER'S FACE-UP CARD	"SUPER-CAUTIOUS" STAND ON 15 OR MORE	"CAUTIOUS" DRAW ON 15 OR LESS; STAND ON 16 OR MORE	"CASINO" DRAW ON 16 OR LESS; STAND ON 17 OR MORE	"BOLD" DRAW ON 17 OR LESS
2, 3, 4, 5	draw on 15 or less; stand on 16 or more	draw on 13 or less; stand on 14 or more	draw on 11 or less; stand on 12 or more	draw on 11 or less; stand on 12 or more
6	draw on 16 or less; stand on 17 or more	draw on 16 or less; stand on 17 or more	draw on 11 or less; stand on 12 or more	draw on 11 or less; stand on 12 or more
7, 8, Ace	draw on 16 or less; stand on 17 or more	draw on 16 or less; stand on 17 or more	draw on 16 or less; stand on 17 or more	draw on 11 or less; stand on 12 or more
9, Ten-Value Cards	draw on 16 or less; stand on 17 or more	draw on 16 or less; stand on 17 or more	draw on 14 or less; stand on 15 or more	draw on 11 or less; stand on 12 or more

Note: the strategy in the above table and previous sections applies to unique totals only. The strategy for soft hands is considered later.

COMPARISON OF THE STRATEGIES FOR THE HOME AND CASINO GAMES

If the home-game dealer always follows the casino strategy, the two games are almost exactly the same. The one important difference is that ties pay the dealer in the home game. When the home-game dealer follows the casino strategy, the player's strategy is similar to the strategy for the casino game described in Chapter 2. In particular, when the dealer's face-up card is a four through eight, inclusive, or an ace, the strategies are identical. Otherwise, the home player tends to stand more than the casino player. For example, when the dealer's face-up card is a two or three, the home player stands on all totals of 12 or more while the casino player also draws on 12. In addition, when the dealer's face-up card is a nine or ten-value card, the home player draws on 14 or less and stands on 15 or more while the casino player also draws on 15 or 16.

The fact that the home player should lie low more often than the casino player may surprise many people. Frequently home players feel that since the dealer takes ties, they cannot be satisfied with low totals and must draw strenuously. As card expert John Crawford says:[2]

"Because ties pay the dealer you should often draw in the home game when you would stand in the casino game. Theoretically, there is a difference of one point. That is, if you would stand on 16 in the casino game, you would hit 16 and need 17 to stand in the home game."

In fairness to Mr. Crawford it should be pointed out that he is referring to the home game in general and not the specific case where the dealer follows the casino strategy. Nevertheless, the type of logic used in the above quotation is quite common.

The reason for the greater tendency to stand pat in the home game is easy to follow. Suppose the player stands on a total of 16 or less. The player will lose unless the dealer busts. The probability that the dealer busts, however, is the same in the casino and home game. On the other hand, suppose the player draws on a total of 16 or less. Since ties pay the dealer, his draw will be less effective in the home game. (For example, suppose the player has a total of 16 and the dealer has a 20. In the home game the player must draw a five to help himself while in the casino game both a four and a five will help.) Thus in the home game standing is just as effective as in the casino game and drawing is less effective.

Drawing and standing on unique totals is probably the single most important aspect of the player's strategy. Yet in the casino game only about 10% of the work was devoted to this problem, the remainder going to doubling down, splitting pairs, and other problems. The home game is considerably more complicated than the casino game and would probably take at least three times as long to analyze completely. Because of limitations of time and energy, only drawing and standing strategy has been given the full mathematical treatment. While the other problems discussed below have been examined from a mathematical point of view, complete solutions have not been obtained. As a result, the final recommendations must be based in part on intuition and opinion.

THE PLAYER'S STRATEGY FOR DRAWING AND STANDING ON SOFT HANDS

Soft hands are frequently good starting points for obtaining five cards not exceeding 21. Consequently, the following recommendations include this consideration:

1. Always draw on soft hands of four or more cards. For example, if the player has 2 fours, 1 two, and 1 ace for soft 21, he should draw. The reason is that the player cannot fail to obtain five cards not exceeding 21 and be paid off at 2 to 1.

2. Always draw on three-card soft totals of 19 or less. For example, the player with 2 fours and an ace should draw. Do not draw on a three-card soft total of 20 unless the dealer's face-up card is a ten-value card. In this situation the dealer has an unusually high chance of holding 20 and beating the player who stands. Never draw on a three-card soft total of 21.

3. Always stand on two-card soft totals of 19 or more. Draw on two-card soft totals of 18 or less with the following two exceptions: (1) if the dealer has a six showing and can be predicted to stand on 16, the player also should stand on two-card soft 17 and 18; (2) if the dealer has a seven showing and can be predicted to stand on 17, the player also should stand on two-card soft 18. The two exceptions above provide an excellent opportunity for bluffing. Let us suppose, for example, that the dealer has a six showing, and the player has a soft 17 consisting of a six up and an ace in the hole. The dealer is likely to figure the player for 16 or less and stand pat with a ten-value card in the hole. Since the dealer has a ten-value card in the hole over 30% of the time, this bluff frequently pays off.

THE PLAYER'S STRATEGY FOR DOUBLING DOWN

Doubling down is less advantageous in the home game than in the casino. An important reason for doubling down in the casino is to get more money on the table when the dealer has a poor card showing. ("Hit him when he's down!") This reason applies in the home game but with less force. Since the dealer takes ties and has a flexible strategy, he is never really "down." Consequently, the player should double down less often in the home game. The following strategy is recommended:

1. Always double down on 11 when the dealer's face-up card is a seven or less but not an ace.

2. If the rules permit, double down on 10 when the dealer's face-up card is a seven or less but not an ace.

3. Never double down on soft hands even if the rules permit this strategy.

4. If the dealer's face-up card is an eight, doubling down on 11 and 10 *may* be slightly advantageous. If the dealer's face-up card is a five or six, doubling down on 9 also may be worthwhile.

THE PLAYER'S STRATEGY FOR SPLITTING PAIRS

Because the dealer takes ties and has a flexible strategy, splitting pairs, like doubling down, is less effective in the home game. The following strategy is recommended:

ACES

Aces should always be split. This is true assuming that a ten-value card and a split ace constitute ordinary 21 only. The advantage in splitting aces is much greater, of course, if this hand is a natural. Aces should be split despite the fact that two aces are the best possible start towards five cards not exceeding 21. However, a single ace is not a bad start either, and the large number of ten-value cards in the deck make 1 or 11 a far superior starting point than 2 or 12.

TEN-VALUE CARDS

Ten-value cards should never be split. This statement holds even if an ace and a split ten-value card form a natural. Twenty is simply too good a hand to break up.

NINES, EIGHTS AND SEVENS

These pairs should be split whenever the pair is higher than the dealer's face-up card. For example, a pair of eights should be split whenever the dealer's face-up card is a seven or less but not an ace. There is only one exception to this rule: nines should not be split if the face-up card is a seven.

SIXES

Sixes should not be split. There is not a great advantage in splitting them in the casino game. Since splitting sixes often leads to totals of 16, and the home-game dealer may stand on 16 and wins ties, splitting is a losing strategy in the home game.

FIVES AND FOURS

These pairs are not split in the casino game, and there is even less advantage in splitting them in the home game.

THREES

Threes should not be split unless the dealer's face-up card is a six. In this situation the player probably should split threes to avoid a very possible 16-16 tie.

TWOS

Twos should never be split. In addition to the general disadvantages of splitting pairs in the home game, 2 twos form a good start on five cards not exceeding 21, while a single two is only a fair start.

THE PLAYER'S STRATEGY IN TRYING FOR BONUSES

In playing for five cards not exceeding 21, the player should always draw on a four-card total of 16 or less. However, he should not draw on a four-card total of 18 or more. When the dealer's face-up card is a seven or higher, including an ace, the player should draw on a four-card total of 17. ("Draw on doubtful 17's.") Otherwise, he should stand on four-card 17.

If six cards not exceeding 21 pays 3 to 1, the player should *never* draw for this bonus unless he is certain to win. In other words, he should stand unless his five-card total is 11 or less. If six cards not exceeding 21 pays 4 to 1, 5 to 1, or 6 to 1, the player should draw on five-card totals of 12 or less, 13 or less, and 14 or less, respectively.

HOW TO PLAY THE DEAL

As a general rule the dealer should draw on 15 or less and stand on 17 or more. He should vary his strategy on 16, thereby keeping the players off-balance. It is suggested that the dealer stand on 16 at least 25% but no more than 75% of the time.

The dealer's action on 16 should be influenced by his own face-up card. If his face-up card is a six or less, the players are more likely to stand on low totals. Therefore, in this situation the dealer should tend to stand on 16. If his face-up card is a seven or higher, including an ace, he should be inclined to draw on 16.

However, the dealer should make the following exceptions to the above general rules:

1. He should stand pat on 15 when *certain* to win 33⅓% or more of the bets of the players who have not busted.

2. He should stand pat on 14 when *certain* to win 40% or more of these bets.

3. If he is *certain* to lose 80% or more of the bets of the players who have not busted by standing pat, he should draw on 17.

4. If he is *certain* to lose 85% or more of these bets by standing pat, he should draw on 18.

Playing the deal well is difficult and requires a great deal of alertness, card sense, and experience. Like the player, the dealer should study the general playing habits of his opponents, the bet sizes, and the players' face-up cards.

THE DEALER'S ADVANTAGE IN THE HOME GAME

The dealer's advantage is an elusive quantity which varies with the rules, the number of players, and the abilities of the players and dealer. Unfortunately, we have not been able to estimate it, even approximately. In our opinion, however, when four or more players engage in the "standard game" described in this chapter, the dealer's advantage lies between 3% and 15%. In other words, in the long run the dealer will win between 3% and 15% of the money bet against him.

THE VALUE OF THE DEAL

The dealer may offer to sell the deal at any time. Many players are anxious to deal, and buying and selling the deal is an important feature of the game.

The deal is terminated when a player has a natural and the dealer does not. The average number of individual hands dealt lies between 21 and 27 depending on the number of players in the game. Consequently, the average value of the deal is at most:

15% x 27 x (the average amount bet per player), or at most *four* times the average amount bet per player.

APPENDIX

Rules on Irregularities

THE HOME GAME

1. After the pack is shuffled and cut the dealer turns up the top card, shows it to all the players, and (except when the card is an ace) places it face up at the bottom of the pack. This is known as "burning a card." If the top card is an ace, the pack is reshuffled and cut, and the burning procedure is repeated. The dealer pays no monetary penalty for failing to burn a card. However, he can be required to shuffle the undealt cards and burn a card before continuing the deal.

2. If a player fails to receive his first card, he can ask for the next undealt card. However, if any players have already received their second card, the player not dealt in must withdraw his bet and drop out of the hand.

3. If a player's first *two* cards are dealt face up, he may drop out of the hand.

4. Any player who stands must expose his hole card as soon as the dealer stands or goes over 21. The player mistakenly standing on a total greater than 21 must pay the dealer double his bet as a penalty. (Note that if the player busts, he is not required to show his hole card.)

5. If the player receives an extra card in the first round of the deal, he may choose which card to keep or keep both as the first cards in two separate hands. However, he cannot play the cards together in the same hand.

6. If the player receives an extra card in the second round of dealing, he may choose which card to keep.

7. If a player who stands is given another card by mistake, he may keep the card. If the card is refused, it

is placed at the bottom of the pack and may not be claimed by the next player.

8. If a card is turned face up in the pack, the player receiving it may refuse it.

9. If the dealer fails to announce a natural before the draw, his hand counts as *ordinary 21* only.

10. An irregularity must be discovered before the bet is settled. Otherwise, the penalty is *not* applied.

THE CASINO GAME

The professional casino dealers rarely make mistakes, and, therefore, the problem of irregularities in the casino game is not very important. Furthermore, since the dealer's strategy is fixed, he is not hurt by the player who fails to turn up his hole cards when going over 21. The only penalty for an irregularity arises when the dealer fails to announce a natural before the draw. In this situation the natural counts as *ordinary 21* only.

References

1. Culbertson, E., Morehead, A. H., and Mott-Smith, G., *Culbertson's Card Games Complete*, The Greystone Press, New York, 1952.

2. Crawford, J. R., *How to Be a Consistent Winner in the Most Popular Card Games*, Doubleday and Company, Inc., Garden City, N.Y., 1953.

3. MacDougall, M., *MacDougall on Dice and Cards*, Coward-McCann, New York, 1944.

4. Scarne, J., *Scarne on Cards*, Crown Publishers, New York, 1949.

5. Scarne, J., and Rawson, C., *Scarne on Dice*, Military Service Publishing Company, Harrisburg, Pa., 1945.

6. Morehead, A. H., Frey, R. L., and Mott-Smith, G., *The New Complete Hoyle*, Garden City Books, Garden City, N.Y., 1956.

7. Morehead, A. H., "How to Win $100 a Week Gambling," *Esquire*, February 1957, p. 51.

8. Le Myre, G., *Le Baccara*, Hermann & Compagnie, Paris, 1935.

9. Culbertson, E., Morehead, A. H., and Mott-Smith, G., *Culbertson's Hoyle*, The Greystone Press, New York, 1950.

10. Baldwin, R. R., Cantey, W. E., Maisel, H., and McDermott, J. P., "The Optimum Strategy in Blackjack," *Journal of the*

American Statistical Association, Volume 51, pp. 429-439, September 1956.

11. Morgenstern, O., and Von Neumann, J., *The Theory of Games and Economic Behavior*, Princeton University Press, Princeton, N.J., 1944.

SUMMARY STRATEGY CHART

(See next page for explanation.)

DRAW OR STAND STRATEGY

Player's Hand / Dealer's Up-Card	2	3	4	5	6	7	8	9	10 (J Q K)	A
17-21	STAND	STAND	STAND	STAND	STAND	STAND	STAND	STAND	STAND	STAND
16	STAND	STAND	STAND	STAND	STAND	GO	GO	GO	GO	GO
15	STAND	STAND	STAND	STAND	STAND	GO	GO	GO	GO	GO
14	STAND	STAND	STAND	STAND	STAND	GO	GO	GO	GO	GO
13	STAND	STAND	STAND	STAND	STAND	GO	GO	GO	GO	GO
12	GO	GO	STAND	STAND	STAND	GO	GO	GO	GO	GO
11 less	GO	GO	GO	GO	GO	GO	GO	GO	GO	GO

DOUBLING DOWN STRATEGY

Player's Hand / Dealer's Up-Card	2	3	4	5	6	7	8	9	10 (J Q K)	A
12 more										
11	DOUBLE	DOUBLE	DOUBLE	DOUBLE	DOUBLE	DOUBLE	DOUBLE	DOUBLE	DOUBLE	
10	DOUBLE	DOUBLE	DOUBLE	DOUBLE	DOUBLE	DOUBLE	DOUBLE			
9	DOUBLE	DOUBLE	DOUBLE	DOUBLE	DOUBLE					
8 less										

SPLITTING PAIRS STRATEGY

Player's Hand / Dealer's Up-Card	2	3	4	5	6	7	8	9	10 (J Q K)	A
A's & 8's	SPLIT	SPLIT	SPLIT	SPLIT	SPLIT	SPLIT	SPLIT	SPLIT	SPLIT	SPLIT
9's	SPLIT	SPLIT	SPLIT	SPLIT	SPLIT		SPLIT	SPLIT		
7's & 6's	SPLIT	SPLIT	SPLIT	SPLIT	SPLIT	SPLIT				
3's & 2's	SPLIT	SPLIT	SPLIT	SPLIT	SPLIT	SPLIT				
10's 5's & 4's										

SPECIAL DETACHABLE SUMMARY FOR CASINO REFERENCE

This page may be torn out easily and carried in the player's pocket.

The chart on the preceding page summarizes the best strategy for casino play. The experienced player should concentrate entirely on the chart, while the inexperienced player should first master the simplified strategy described at the bottom of this page.

Blackjack is a very fast game and delays of any kind meet the disapproval of the dealer and other players. Consequently, the player should study the chart (or simplified strategy) carefully before sitting down at the blackjack table, and, once seated, use it for brief references only. If longer references are required, the player can always withdraw temporarily from the game.

THE SIMPLIFIED STRATEGY

1. When the dealer's face-up card is a seven or higher or an ace, draw on 16 or less and stand on 17 or more. When the dealer's face-up card is a six or less, draw on 11 or less and stand on 12 or more. Count the ace as 1 unless counting it as 11 will make your total 18, 19, 20, or 21.

2. Always double down on 10 and 11, but never double down on any other totals.

3. Always split aces and eights, but never split any other pair.

THE FOUR HORSEMEN OF ABERDEEN

Left to Right: James McDermott, Wilbert Cantey, Herbert
Maisel and Roger Baldwin. Photo taken October 2007

DON'T PLAY BLACKJACK—except for fun
—unless you have read this book!

Four bright young mathematicians spent over
a thousand man-hours figuring the odds on this
popular card game (call it Twenty-One or
Blackjack, as you will), and they came up with
a concise and readable handbook that cuts the
dealer's odds from the four or five percent
accepted by many of today's leading card experts to *approximately six-tenths of one percent.*

Both "casino" and "home games" are covered,
in their infinite number of rules and variations.
Three charts cover the best strategy for hitting,
the best strategy for splitting pairs, the best
strategy for going down double. A final summary chart may be removed for use by the
player either in casino or in home play.

Note for those who like statistics: This material adds up
to twelve years of careful computations on desk calculators, since each of the four authors devoted three years
of off-duty time in the Army to figuring the odds that
make this the most accurate and original book ever
written about Blackjack.

M. BARROWS AND COMPANY
425 Fourth Avenue, New York 16, New York

FREE BOOK!
TAKE ADVANTAGE OF THIS OFFER NOW!

The book is **free**; the shipping is **free**. Truly, no obligation. Oops, we forgot. You also get a **free** catalog. **And a $10 off coupon!!** Mail in coupon below to get your free book or go to **www.cardozabooks.com** and click on the red OFFER button.

WHY ARE WE GIVING YOU THIS BOOK?
Why not? No, seriously, after more than 27 years as the world's foremost publisher of gaming books, we really appreciate your business. Take this **free** book as our thank you for being our customer; we're sure we'll see more of you!

THIS OFFER GETS EVEN BETTER & BETTER!
You'll get a **FREE** catalog of all our products—over 200 to choose from—and get this: you'll also get a **$10 FREE** coupon good for purchase of <u>any</u> product in our catalog! Our offer is pretty simple. Let me sum it up for you:
  1. Order your **FREE** book
  2. Shipping of your book is **FREE!***
  3. Get a **FREE** catalog (over 200 items—and more on the web)
  4. You <u>also</u> get a **$10 OFF** coupon good for anything we sell
  5. Enjoy your free book and **WIN**!

CHOOSE YOUR FREE BOOK
Choose one book from any in the Basics of Winning Series (15 choices): Baccarat, Bingo, Blackjack, Bridge, Caribbean Stud Poker and Let it Ride, Chess, Craps, Hold'em, Horseracing, Keno, Lotto/Lottery, Poker, Roulette, Slots, Sports Betting, Video Poker.

Or choose one book from here: Internet Hold'em Poker, Crash Course in Beating Texas Hold'em, Poker Talk, Poker Tournament Tips from the Pros, or Bobby Baldwin's Winning Poker Secrets.

When you order your free book by Internet, enter the coupon code **NAME**.

HURRY! GET YOUR FREE BOOK NOW!
USE THIS COUPON OR GO TO OUR WEBSITE!

YES! Send me my **FREE** book! I understand there is no obligation! Send coupon to: <u>Cardoza Publishing</u>, P.O. Box 98115, Las Vegas, NV 89193. <u>No</u> phone calls please.

Free book by website: www.cardozabooks.com (click on red OFFER button)

*Shipping is FREE to U.S. (Sorry, due to very high ship costs, we cannot offer this outside the U.S. However, we still have good news for foreign customers: Spend $25 or more with us and we'll include that free book for you anyway!)

WRITE IN FREE BOOK HERE _____

Name _____

Address _____

City _____ State _____ Zip _____

Email Address* _____ Coupon Code: <u>PLAYBJ</u>

*Get our FREE newsletter and special offers when you provide your email. Your information is <u>protected</u> by our privacy guarantee: We've been in business 27 years and do NOT and never have sold customer info. One coupon per address or per person only. Offer subject to cancellation at any time.

NEW BLACKJACK TITLES
BOOKS YOU MUST HAVE

THE BLACKJACK SHUFFLE TRACKER'S COOKBOOK
by Arnold Snyder
$49.95

In this 110-page professional report, Arnold Snyder reveals techniques never-before disclosed on the advanced and dangerous form of card counting known as shuffle tracking. These powerful techniques, known only to a few professional players, are way below the casino radar and allows players to use their winning skills long before the casinos ever get wind that there is an advantage player taking their money.

Included are numerous practice and testing methods for learning shuffle tracking, methods for analyzing and comparing the profit potential of various shuffles, the cost of errors; and much, much more. The hard data is organized into simple charts, and carefully explained. Note: If you are not currently a card counter, this book is not the place to start as shuffle tracking is not easy. This is for serious players only.

THE CARD COUNTER'S GUIDE
TO CASINO SURVEILLANCE
by D.V. Cellini
$99.99

Learning the subtleties of playing winning blackjack undetected is an extremely difficult skill. It's hard enough to fool the casino employees you can see—dealers, floormen, pit bosses, and casino managers—but then there's the "eye," the behind-the-scenes surveillance department, with its biometric-identifying software along with the surveillance agents themselves. But now, for the first time ever, a long-time surveillance agent with vast experience and knowledge has emerged from the deep and dark recesses and exposed the inner workings to the light of scrutiny.

This 135-page special report is packed with inside advice on solo and team-play tactics; how to fly below the radar screen; how to confuse the agents and software; successful camouflage and counter-offensive techniques; and even sure-fire ways to get busted. This is a mighty weapon in any card-counter's arsenal—and it's fascinating reading for anyone interested in how casinos really work.

Order now at 1-800-577-WINS or go online to: www.cardozabooks.com

Win at Blackjack Without Counting Cards!!!
Multiple Deck 1, 2, 3 Non-Counter - Breakthrough in Blackjack!!!

BEAT MULTIPLE DECK BLACKJACK WITHOUT COUNTING CARDS!
You heard right! Now, for the **first time ever**, win at multiple deck blackjack **without counting cards**! Until I developed the Cardoza Multiple Deck Non-Counter (the 1,2,3 Strategy), I thought it was impossible. Don't be intimidated anymore by four, six or eight deck games - for **you have the advantage**. It doesn't matter how many decks they use, for this easy-to-use and proven strategy keeps you **winning - with the odds**!

EXCITING STRATEGY - ANYONE CAN WIN! - We're excited about this strategy for it allows anyone at all, against any number of decks, to have the **advantage** over any casino in the world in a multiple deck game. You don't count cards, you don't need a great memory, you don't need to be good at math - you just need to know the **winning secrets** of the 1,2,3 Multiple Deck Non-Counter and use but a **little effort** to win $$$.

SIMPLE BUT EFFECTIVE! - Now the answer is here. This strategy is so **simple**, yet so **effective**, you will be amazed. With a **minimum of effort**, this remarkable strategy, which we also call the 1,2,3 (as easy as 1,2,3), allows you to win without studiously following cards. Drink, converse with your fellow players or dealer - they'll never suspect that you can **beat the casino**!

PERSONAL GUARANTEE - And you have my personal **guarantee of satisfaction**, 100% money back! This breakthrough strategy is my personal research and is guaranteed to give you the edge! If for any reason you're not satisfied, send back the materials unused within 30 days for a full refund.

BE A LEISURELY WINNER! - If you just want to play a **leisurely game** yet have the expectation of winning, the answer is here. Not as powerful as a card counting strategy, but **powerful enough to make you a winner** - with the odds!!!

EXTRA BONUS! - Complete listing of all options and variations at blackjack and how they affect the player. ($5.00 Value!)

EXTRA, EXTRA BONUS!! - Not really a bonus since we can't sell you the strategy without protecting you against getting barred. The 1,000 word essay, "How to Disguise the Fact That You're an Expert," and the 1,500 word "How Not To Get Barred," are also included free. ($15.00 Value)
To Order, send ~~$75~~ $50 (plus postage and handling) by check or money order to:
Cardoza Publishing, P.O. Box 98115, Las Vegas, NV 89193

$25 OFF! (Only $50 With This Coupon!)
Yes! I want to be a winner at blackjack! Please rush me the **Cardoza Multiple Deck Non-Counter** (The **1,2,3 Strategy**). I understand that all the two bonus essays, and the "Options and Variations" Charts all will be included **absolutely free**! Enclosed is a check or money order for $50 (plus postage and handling) made out to:
Cardoza Publishing, P.O. Box 98115, Las Vegas, NV 89193
MC/Visa/Amex Orders Toll-Free in U.S. & Canada, 1-800-577-WINS
Include $5.00 postage/handling for U.S. orders; $10.00 for Can/Mex; HI/AK and other countries $15.00. Outside U.S., money order payable in U.S. dollars on U.S. bank only.

NAME_____

ADDRESS_____

CITY _____ STATE _____ ZIP _____
MC/Visa/Amex Orders By Mail
MC/Visa/Amex # _____ Phone _____

Exp. Date _____ Signature _____
Order Now! 30 Day Money Back Guarantee!
PLAYBJ

WIN MONEY AT BLACKJACK! SPECIAL OFFER!
THE CARDOZA BASE COUNT STRATEGY

Finally, a count strategy has been developed which allows the average player to play blackjack like a **pro**! Actually, this strategy isn't new. The Cardoza Base Count Strategy has been used successfully by graduates of the Cardoza School of Blackjack for years. But **now**, for the **first time**, this "million dollar" strategy, which was only available previously to those students attending the school, is available to **you**!

FREE VACATIONS! A SECOND INCOME? - You bet! Once you learn this strategy, you will have the skills to **consistently win big money** at blackjack. The longer you play, the more you make. The casino's bankroll is yours for the taking.

BECOME AN EXPERT IN TWO DAYS - Why struggle over complicated strategies that aren't as powerful? In just **two days or less**, you can learn the Cardoza Base Count and be among the best blackjack players. Friends will look up to you in awe - for you will be a **big winner** at blackjack.

BEAT ANY SINGLE OR MULTIPLE DECK GAME - We show you how, with just a **little effort**, you can effectively beat any single or multiple deck game. You'll learn how to count cards, how to use advanced betting and playing strategies, how to make money on insurance bets, and much, much, more in this 6,000 word, chart-filled strategy package.

SIMPLE TO USE, EASY TO MASTER - You too can win! The **power** of the Cardoza Base Count strategy is not only in its **computer-proven** winning results but also in its **simplicity**. Many beginners who thought card counting was too difficult have given the Cardoza Base Count the acid test - they have **won consistently** in casinos around the world. The Cardoza Base Count strategy is designed so that **any player** can win under practical casino conditions. **No need** for a mathematical mind or photographic memory. **No need** to be bogged down by calculations. Keep **only one number** in your head at any time. The casinos will never suspect that you're a counter.

DOUBLE BONUS!! - **Rush** your order in **now**, for we're also including, **absolutely free**, the 1,000 and 1,500 word essays, "How to Disguise the Fact that You're an Expert", and "How Not to Get Barred". Among other **inside information** contained here, you'll learn about the psychology of the pit bosses, how they spot counters, how to project a losing image, role playing, and other skills to maximize your profit potential.

As an **introductory offer to readers of this book**, the Cardoza Base Count Strategy, which has netted graduates of the Cardoza School of Blackjack **substantial sums** of **money**, is offered here for **only** $50! To order, send $50 by check or money order to: Cardoza Publishing, P.O. Box 98115, Las Vegas, NV 89193

WIN MONEY PLAYING BLACKJACK!
MAIL THIS COUPON NOW!

Yes, I want to **win big money** at blackjack. Please **rush** me the Cardoza Base Count Strategy. I understand that the Double Bonus essays are included **absolutely free**. Enclosed is a check or money order for $50 (plus postage and handling) made out to:
Cardoza Publishing, P.O. Box 98115, Las Vegas, NV 89193
Call Toll-Free in U.S. & Canada, 1-800-577-WINS

Include $5.00 postage/handling for U.S. orders; $10.00 for Can/Mex; HI/AK and other countries $15.00. Outside U.S., money order payable in U.S. dollars on U.S. bank only.

NAME_____

ADDRESS_____

CITY _____ STATE _____ ZIP _____

Order Now to Win! 30 Day Money Back Guarantee!
PLAYBJ

CARDOZA SCHOOL OF BLACKJACK
- Home Instruction Course - $200 OFF! -

At last, after years of secrecy, the **previously unreleased** lesson plans, strategies and playing tactics formerly available only to members of the Cardoza School of Blackjack are now available to the general public - and at substantial savings. **Now**, you can **learn at home,** and at your own convenience. Like the full course given at the school, the home instruction course goes **step-by-step** over the winning concepts. We'll take you from layman to **pro.**

MASTER BLACKJACK - Learn what it takes to be a **master player.** Be a **powerhouse,** play with confidence, impunity, and **with the odds** on your side. Learn to be a **big winner** at blackjack.

MAXIMIZE WINNING SESSIONS - You'll **learn how** to take a good winning session and make a **blockbuster** out of it, but just as important, you'll learn to cut your losses. Learn exactly when to end a session. We cover everything from the psychological and emotional aspects of play to altered playing conditions (through the **eye of profitability**) to protection of big wins. The advice here could be worth **hundreds (or thousands) of dollars** in one session alone. Take our guidelines seriously.

ADVANCED STRATEGIES - You'll learn the latest in advanced winning strategies. Learn about the **ten-factor**, the **Ace-factor**, the effects of rules variations, how to protect against dealer blackjacks, the winning strategies for single and multiple deck games and how each affects you; the **true count**, the multiple deck true count variations, and much, much more. And, of course, you'll receive the full Cardoza Base Count Strategy package.

$200 OFF - LIMITED OFFER - The Cardoza School of Blackjack home instruction course, retailed at $295 (or $895 if taken at the school) is available here for just $95.

DOUBLE BONUS! - **Rush** your order in **now**, for we're also including, **absolutely free,** the 1,000 and 1,500 word essays, "How to Disguise the Fact that You're an Expert", and "How Not to Get Barred". Among other **inside information** contained here, you'll learn about the psychology of the pit bosses, how they spot counters, how to project a losing image, role playing, and other skills to maximize your profit potential.

To order, send $95 (plus postage and handling) by check or money order to:
Cardoza Publishing, P.O. Box 98115, Las Vegas, NV 89193

SAVE $200!
(regularly $295 - Only $95 with coupon)

Order Now! Be a big winner! Please **rush** me the course by mail. I want to join the thousands of successful graduates **winning big money** at blackjack. I understand that the **Double Bonus** essays and **free** book will be included **absolutely free.**
Enclosed is a check or money order for $95 (plus postage and handling) made out to:
Cardoza Publishing, P.O. Box 98115, Las Vegas, NV 89193
Call Toll-Free in U.S. & Canada, 1-800-577-WINS
Include $5.00 postage/handling for U.S. orders; $10.00 for Can/Mex; HI/AK and other countries $15.00. Outside U.S., money order payable in U.S. dollars on U.S. bank only.

NAME_____

ADDRESS_____

CITY _____ STATE _____ ZIP _____

Order Now to Win! 30 Day Money Back Guarantee! PLAYBJ

5 PROFESSIONAL REPORTS TO TURN AMATEUR CARD COUNTERS TO PROS

NOT FOR BEGINNERS—FOR CARD COUNTERS ONLY

NEW AND REVISED! - These are the **groundbreaking** reports relied upon by **professional blackjack players** for more than 25 years. And now, in late 2004, they are completely updated! This is a **very big event** for winning and pro blackjack players.

THE LEGEND REVEALS HIS SECRETS - These professional strategies are the personal work of Arnold Snyder, **legendary** blackjack player and guru to thousands of serious players. Snyder, **one of the greatest players** in history and a member of the **Blackjack Hall of Fame**, is the author of nine books and advanced strategies including his national best-seller, Blackbelt in Blackjack.

THE PROFESSIONAL COUNTERS SECRET STRATEGIES - Start **winning** by applying the strongest betting strategy with the lowest risk. Good for all valid counting systems, some of the technical questions answered are:
- What's my advantage if the dealer deals out 4 1/2 decks instead of just 4 decks?
- Should I raise my bet at a count of +3 or +4?
- Can I beat the game if I use a betting spread of 1-to-4 units, or do I need 1-to-8?
- What's the best betting strategy if I only have $1,000 and the minimum bet is $10?
- What's my win rate if I quit the table when the count goes negative?
- What's my win rate if the house uses eight decks instead of six?

You **don't need** to run computer simulations to get the answers, and you don't need a degree in probability and statistics. You simply need a set of charts where you can look up the answers—the math has already been worked out. **Accurate for all counting systems** and any size bankroll, each report is 64 pages, with 44 pages of charts. There are five separate reports for games being dealt with 1, 2, 4, 6, and 8 decks. With any betting spread, the charts show the fluctuations you can expect in an hour of play, ten hours, a hundred hours and more, so you can estimate your **best approach** to any game based on your actual bankroll. Get just the Reports that cover the games you currently play in, or get them all (and save $$$) to **be prepared** for any blackjack game anywhere.

Beat the 1-Deck Game: $25	**Beat the 6-Deck Game:** $25
Beat the 2-Deck Game: $25	**Beat the 8-Deck Game:** $25
Beat the 4-Deck Game: $25	**All five reports:** $95 (You save $30.00!)

To order, send $95 for all 5 reports (or $25 per report)—plus postage and handling to:
Cardoza Publishing, P.O. Box 98115, Las Vegas, NV 89193

WIN MONEY PLAYING BLACKJACK!
MAIL THIS COUPON NOW!

Yes, Get me these reports right away. Please **rush** me the **Beat the Deck Reports** listed below. Enclosed is a check or money order for $95 for the full set of reports (or $25 per report)—plus postage and handling made out to:
Cardoza Publishing, P.O. Box 98115, Las Vegas, NV 89193

Call Toll-Free in U.S. & Canada, 1-800-577-WINS

All Reports $95 ___ 1-Deck ___ 2-Deck ___ 4-Deck ___ 6-Deck ___ 8-Deck ___

Include $5.00 postage/handling for U.S. orders; $10.00 for Can/Mex; HI/AK and other countries $15.00. Outside U.S., money order payable in U.S. dollars on U.S. bank only.

NAME_____

ADDRESS_____

CITY _____ STATE _____ ZIP _____

Order Now to Be a Winner! 30 Day Money Back Guarantee! PLAYBJ

POWERFUL WINNING POKER SIMULATIONS
A MUST FOR SERIOUS PLAYERS WITH A COMPUTER!
IBM compatible CD ROM Win 95, 98, 2000, NT, ME, XP

These incredible full color poker simulations are the best method to improve your game. Computer opponents play like real players. All games let you set the limits and rake and have fully programmable players, plus stat tracking, and Hand Analyzer for starting hands. MIke Caro, the world's foremost poker theoretician says, "Amazing... a steal for under $500... get it, it's great." Includes free phone support. "Smart Advisor" gives expert advice for every play!

1. TURBO TEXAS HOLD'EM FOR WINDOWS - $59.95. Choose which players, and how many (2-10) you want to play, create loose/tight games, and control check-raising, bluffing, position, sensitivity to pot odds, and more! Also, instant replay, pop-up odds, Professional Advisor keeps track of play statistics. Free bonus: Hold'em Hand Analyzer analyzes all 169 pocket hands in detail and their win rates under any conditions you set. Caro says this "hold'em software is the most powerful ever created." Great product!

2. TURBO SEVEN-CARD STUD FOR WINDOWS - $59.95. Create any conditions of play; choose number of players (2-8), bet amounts, fixed or spread limit, bring-in method, tight/loose conditions, position, reaction to board, number of dead cards, and stack deck to create special conditions. Features instant replay. Terrific stat reporting includes analysis of starting cards, 3-D bar charts, and graphs. Play interactively and run high speed simulation to test strategies. Hand Analyzer analyzes starting hands in detail. Wow!

3. TURBO OMAHA HIGH-LOW SPLIT FOR WINDOWS - $59.95. Specify any playing conditions; betting limits, number of raises, blind structures, button position, aggressiveness/passiveness of opponents, number of players (2-10), types of hands dealt, blinds, position, board reaction, and specify flop, turn, and river cards! Choose opponents and use provided point count or create your own. Statistical reporting, instant replay, pop-up odds high speed simulation to test strategies, amazing Hand Analyzer, and much more!

4. TURBO OMAHA HIGH FOR WINDOWS - $59.95. Same features as above, but tailored for Omaha High only. Caro says program is "an electrifying research tool...it can clearly be worth thousands of dollars to any serious player." A must for Omaha High players.

5. TURBO 7 STUD 8 OR BETTER - $59.95. Brand new with all the features you expect from the Wilson Turbo products: the latest artificial intelligence, instant advice and exact odds, play versus 2-7 opponents, enhanced data charts that can be exported or printed, the ability to fold out of turn and immediately go to the next hand, ability to peek at opponents hand, optional warning mode that warns you if a play disagrees with the advisor, and automatic mode that runs up to 50 tests unattended. Tough computer players vary their styles for a great game.

6. TOURNAMENT TEXAS HOLD'EM - $39.95

Set-up for tournament practice and play, this realistic simulation pits you against celebrity look-alikes. Tons of options let you control tournament size with 10 to 300 entrants, select limits, ante, rake, blind structures, freezeouts, number of rebuys and competition level of opponents. Pop-up status report shows how you're doing vs. the competition. Save tournaments in progress to play again later. Additional feature allows quick folds on finished hands.

Order now at 1-800-577-WINS or go online to: www.cardozabooks.com

FREE!
Poker & Gaming Magazines

www.cardozabooks.com

3 GREAT REASONS TO VISIT NOW!

1. FREE GAMING MAGAZINES
Go online now and read all about the exciting world of poker, gambling, and online gaming. Our magazines are packed with tips, expert strategies, tournament schedules and results, gossip, news, contests, polls, exclusive discounts on hotels, travel, and more to our readers, prepublication book discounts, free-money bonuses for online sites, and words of wisdom from the world's top experts and authorities. Also, you can opt-in for Avery Cardoza's free email newsletters.

2. MORE THAN 200 BOOKS TO MAKE YOU A WINNER
We are the world's largest publisher of gaming and gambling books and represent a who's who of the greatest players and writers on poker, gambling, chess, back-gammon, and other games. With more than nine million books sold, we know what our customers want. Trust us.

3. THIS ONE IS A SURPRISE
Visit us now to get the goods!

So what are you waiting for?

CARDOZA PUBLISHING ONLINE